Boys on th

Sam Grabiner is a playwright and *Boys on the Verge of Tears* is his debut production.

SAM GRABINER

Boys on the Verge of Tears

faber

First published in 2024
by Faber and Faber Limited
The Bindery, 51 Hatton Garden
London, EC1N 8HN

Typeset by Brighton Gray
Printed and bound in the UK by CPI Group (Ltd), Croydon CR0 4YY

A CIP record for this book
is available from the British Library

ISBN 978-0-571-39017-5

Printed and bound in the UK on FSC® certified paper in line with our continuing
commitment to ethical business practices, sustainability and the environment.
For further information see faber.co.uk/environmental-policy

4 6 8 10 9 7 5 3

Boys on the Verge of Tears was first performed at Soho Theatre, London, on 11 April 2024, with the following cast:

Matthew Beard
David Carlyle
Calvin Demba
Tom Espiner
Maanuv Thiara

Director James Macdonald
Set & Costume Designer Ashley Martin-Davis
Lighting Designer Peter Mumford
Sound Designer Ian Dickinson for Autograph
Costume Supervisor Zoë Thomas-Webb
Casting Director Amy Ball
Intimacy and Fight Co-ordinator Enric Ortuño
Production Manager Tom Nickson
Lighting Associate Claire Gerrens
Assistant Director Alex Kampfner
Company Stage Manager Sally McKenna
Deputy Stage Manager Olivia Kerslake
Assistant Stage Manager Jasmine Dittman
Associate Producer Eve Allin

For Sophie

Characters

Father
Boy
Zaid
Callum
Billy Bonkers
Jesse
Ali
Simon
Charlotte
Lola
Jack
Hamza
Fred
Oscar
Owen
Mr Thomas
Ace
Jay
Liam
Jo
Dee
Cal
Milo
Terry
Marty
Sid
Patrick
Kay
Ollie
Vanessa Feltz
Maureen Lip-Man

Hunter
Frank
Oz
Ola
Jamal
Fin
Stepson
Stepfather

BOYS ON THE VERGE OF TEARS

'Does that mean', I said in some bewilderment, 'that we must eat again of the tree of knowledge in order to return to the state of innocence?'

'Of course', he said, 'but that's the final chapter in the history of the world.'

Heinrich von Kleist, *On the Marionette Theatre*

Notes

This play is performed by a company of five actors
(and a sixth for the final page).

All performers are adults
(aside from the sixth on the final page).

Although the play is divided into three Movements, these
should run continuously. No blackouts.

*

A comma (,) on its own line suggests a beat, or a pause,
or a silence of some sort.

An ellipsis (. . .) indicates a trailing off.

A forward slash (/) indicates the point of interruption
by the next speaker.

An en-dash (–) indicates a cutting off.

Sometimes the dialogue splits into columns.
This signifies simultaneous action.

Movement One

A toilet in a public place. Cubicles and urinals and sinks and hand dryers. Somewhere, a bin.
   The Father stands outside a cubicle. He is dressed for a summer's day at the park. From inside the cubicle, we hear the voice of:

Boy I don't need any help.

Father I didn't say you needed help, I just asked if you were doing okay?
   Well?

Boy I'm fine.

Father Good.

   The Father waits, trying to listen.

Boy Stop listening

Father I'm not listening –

Boy I can hear you listening –

Father How can you hear me listening?

Boy You're making that breathing noise

Father What breathing noise

Boy That breathing noise you make when you listen

Father You can't *hear* someone listen –

Boy I can I can I can I can –

Father Okay, okay.
   Sorry. I will stop listening.

Boy Take a step back.

Father What?

Boy Take a step back you're right up against the door.

The Father takes a step away from the cubicle.

Father How's that?

Boy Better.

Father Have you lifted the seat up?

Boy DAD!

Father What?!

Boy Shut up!

Father Don't tell me to shut up!

Boy Don't tell me to lift up the seat!

Father (*softly*) Lift up the seat darling.

We hear the sound of a toilet lid being lifted up.

Good.
    Have you lifted up both?

Boy What do you mean?

Father The lid, and then the seat as well.

Boy Yes of course I've lifted both I'm not stupid!

The sound of a toilet seat being lifted. The Father smiles to himself.

Father Good.

Boy Now what?

Father Do you want me to come / inside I

Boy NO!

Father Okay, okay.
    Unclip your belt.

Boy Obviously.

Father Okay. And now undo the buckle on your shorts and unzip your flies.

We hear this happen.

Good, and now –

Boy Go to the other side of the room.

Father What?

Boy Go to the other side of the room.

Father Why?

Boy Because you're too near.

Father Okay I am moving to the other side of the room.

The Father moves further away.

Now does / your

Boy Further.

The Father walks a little further still.

Father How's this?

Boy Fine.

Father Good. Now. Does your willy reach above the toilet seat?

Boy (*quietly*) I think so.

Father Very good. Now what you need to do is make sure that it's aimed towards the right place.
  Do you understand?

Boy (*very quietly*) Which place.

Father What was that darling?

Boy Aimed where?

Father At the bit with the water.
   Does that make sense?

   The sound of pissing into a toilet bowl.
      The Father stops and listens with pride.
      The pissing stops.

Very good now shake it / so

   The pissing starts again.
      The Father waits.
      The pissing finishes.

Good. Now what you need to do is you need to shake it
a little bit. So if there are any drips on your willy they
come off.
   Good. And then you can close the lid and then reach up
and flush the chain. Are you okay doing that? Because now
you've done all the important bit yourself like a very brave
boy I can come in and flush if you'd / like

Boy No!
   And don't call me a brave boy that's what you call babies.

Father I'm sorry.
   Can you close the lid and flush the chain because
Mummy is waiting for us and we can get an ice cream from
the man in the hat.
   Darling?
   Okay I'm going to come in now because we can't keep
Mummy waiting for us all this / time can we

Boy STOP!

Father (*accidentally stern*) Come on this is ridiculous it's
just a piss let's be done now.

Boy Something went wrong.

Father What do you mean something went wrong?

Boy With the wee.

Father How could something've gone wrong?

Boy I got some on me.

The Father fights back a laugh.

Father Well that's alright mate. Sometimes that happens. And you'll get better and better as you get older.

Boy Don't laugh!

Father I'm not laughing.
Where did it go?
Is it on the floor?

Boy Yes.

Father Well worse things have been on this floor I'm sure.

Boy Like what?

Father . . . Don't worry. Is it anywhere else?

Boy My shoes.

Father Right. That's okay. Do you want to know a little secret?
Well? Do you?

Boy Yes.

Father Sometimes Daddy gets a bit of wee on his shoes too.

Boy That's disgusting.

Father It's not darling it's normal.

Boy You wee on your shoes?

Father Well not / always

Boy You're an adult you shouldn't be weeing on your shoes.

Father Come on out you come let's wash our hands.

Boy It's all over the Green Ranger.

Father Excuse me?

9

Boy I've gotten wee all over the Green Ranger.

The Father tries to process this.

And on the Dinozord and on the Blue Ranger and on the Sabertooth Tiger too.

Realisation.

Father Your T-shirt

Boy Yes of course my T-shirt!

Father comes to the cubicle to open the door.

If you come in here I'm going to SCREAM!

Father Calm down.
You have to come out here and then we can go to Mummy by the swings and she's got a change of T-shirt for you, okay? Then we can have ice cream and then we can go home and we can watch as much *Power Rangers* as you like, how about that?
Well? The Green Ranger, the Blue Ranger, the Unicorn . . .

Boy The Unicorn Thunderzord –

Father The Unicorn Thunderzord, yes. All of it. We can watch all afternoon, how about that?

Boy Dad?

Father Yes?

Boy I need a poo.

The Father makes a silent 'OH MY GOD I WANT TO SCREAM' gesture to himself.

What's the matter?

Father Nothing's the matter.

Boy Then why did you just put your hands in the air and do that scary face?

Father I didn't.

Boy Yes you did I saw you there's a gap in the door don't lie.

Father It's just that Daddy's quite tired.

Boy Tired people sleep they don't make scary faces and throw their hands in the air.

Father Well sometimes they do.

Boy That's strange.

Father People are strange sometimes. Now why don't we go home and you do your poo in the toilet there.

The Father smells something.

Boy Too late.
I want you to go away now. I want you to leave I want Mummy now.

Father Mummy's busy with your sister.

Boy No they'll be done now I want Mummy.

Father I thought you said you were grown up enough to do it by yourself?

Boy (*quietly*) I am.

Father What was that?

Boy I AM!
But you're bad at it.
You're so bad at it and I want Mummy.

Father Well she can't come in here darling this toilet's for boys, remember? And you said you wanted to come into the boys' toilet because you're not a baby any more. And you're not a girl, are you? You're a big boy.

Boy I won't listen to an adult who pisses on his own feet.

The Father takes some time to process this.

Father . . . I don't . . .
I only said that to make you feel –
That's a very naughty word darling you shouldn't use it

Boy *You* did.

Father I know I did and I was wrong.

Boy Not for the first time.

Father Let me come in and help you.

Boy I want Mummy I don't want you to wipe my bum
I want Mummy to wipe my bum

Father She can't come in / here

Boy Why not??

The Father puts his head in his hands and crouches on his knees.

Do tired people put their head in their hands and crouch down on their knees too?

Father Yes. They do. And angry people too.

Boy Get. Mummy.
(*Suddenly very vulnerable.*) Please.

Father This is the last time, you know that?

Boy I know.

Father Big boys have got to grow up, don't they?

The Father leaves, calling out as he goes:

Mum!
(*Off in the distance, to someone.*) Looks like we have a very small boy doing a very big shit in there.

,

The Boy kicks the cubicle door from the inside.

,

Zaid, a slightly older boy, comes in. He is wearing a party hat and eating a packet of crisps.

He goes to a urinal, tucks his crisps under an arm and undoes his trousers, letting his pants and trousers fall to his ankles as he pisses.

Using a urinal is fairly new to him, but he just about knows his way around.

He finishes and moves to the mirrors. He starts eating his crisps again, without washing his hands.

Zaid Boring in there, isn't it?

My party last year was way WAY better. You weren't there because I was at a different school then so we didn't know each other not that we know each other too much now but anyway the old school I was at was definitely worse but the parties were better and there's no way there'd be a party at a sports centre as small as this.

(*Suddenly.*) FUCK!

He giggles.

You've probably heard that I got expelled. Well it's true. I was too clever? Like I was too clever and so the other kids complained and I was like yeah whatever I don't actually care your parties might be quite good but this is actually quite a bad school? My dad said don't worry they're all cunts anyway that's what he said: don't worry son they're all cunts anyway.

Cunt is a bad word you know?

Like a *really* bad word.

Fuck is bad but cunt is like way WAY worse.

You probably don't know any swear words though, do you?

Are you dumb or something?

I know you're in there. Well? Are you dumb?

From inside the same cubicle the Boy has been in, a new voice: Callum's. He's a little older-sounding than the Boy.

Callum No.

Zaid Right I thought you might be dumb because you weren't saying anything.

Callum I'm busy.

Zaid Busy doing a shit?
  Shit's a bad word too but you probably know that one everyone knows that one, not everyone knows cunt though that's more rare. Like a tiger or something. Yeah. Shit is like a pigeon, like everyone sees pigeons they're just hanging about aren't they in the park and stuff. But a tiger! WOW! A tiger people go on holiday for. Cunt is rare, cunt is a rare magical tiger you have to go ages away to get a look at . . . you'd have to go to like . . . France or something to see that.

Callum There aren't tigers in France

Zaid Yes there are

Callum No there are not they're found in three different kinds of places: grasslands, jungles and rainforests.

Zaid Rubbish.

Callum No not rubbish. They wouldn't be found in France on account of the landscape. They'd be found in India and China and then sometimes in a place called Indo . . . Indo . . . Indo something.

Zaid Shut up.

Callum Maybe Indiachina? Or Indichina. No that's not right. It's Inda . . . Inder –

Zaid SHUT UP.

Callum Okay.

  The sound of the toilet flushing.

Zaid What do you know about anything anyway.

14

The cubicle door opens, revealing Callum.
He is dressed in a head-to-toe tiger costume, face paint and everything.

Callum Hi.

Zaid Hi.
Guess you do sort of know about tigers don't you.

Callum They're my favourite animal.

Callum moves over to the taps and washes his hands methodically. Counting the seconds under his breath.

Zaid You want a crisp?

Callum I'm saving space for cake.

Zaid This party is SO BAD.

Callum I like it –

Zaid Really? Why?

Callum I like Billy Bonkers.

Zaid Oh my GOD how old are you, five?

Callum I like when he ties the balloons into animals. He gave me a tiger once.

Zaid My dad says Billy Bonkers is a paedo.

Callum What's paedo?

Zaid I don't know I think it's got something to do with dinosaurs? But it's definitely not good.

Callum I like dinosaurs.

Zaid Well maybe you're a paedo then.

Callum I hope not.

Zaid Are you scared of me?

Callum just looks at him.

I think you're scared of me.

Callum I'm scared of quite a lot of things.

Zaid I don't have many friends.

Callum It takes time. That's what my mum says.

Zaid You're quite tall for our year.

Callum Thanks. So are you.

Zaid Not really.

Callum Yeah not really I was just saying that to be nice.

Zaid takes out a huge kitchen knife.

Zaid I stole this would you like to play with it?

Callum stands there. Frozen.

It was next to the cake and nobody was watching they were all busy looking at Billy Bonkers do his weird thing where he piles all the presents into the birthday boy's arms so I thought it'd be fun if we played with this in here instead.

You scared or something?

Callum That's not allowed.

Zaid Doesn't matter nobody saw me.

Callum It's wrong to steal.

Zaid We're not stealing because I'll put it back after so we're just borrowing.

And it's good to share, remember.

You really are very tall for our year. Your arms are so long and I like your skin.

Callum Thank you.

Zaid Why are you looking at me like that?

Callum Like what?

Zaid Like I'm a baddy.

Callum Don't know.

Zaid Would you like to hold it.

Callum shakes his head.

Go on I promise it's fun you should hold it.

Zaid holds the knife out.

I like your hair it looks really cool for a tiger.

Callum takes the knife.

Callum Wow.
It's.
Wow.

Zaid Cool huh?

Callum nods.

Callum I feel like a samurai.

Zaid What's a samurai?

Callum It's a special Japanese fighter

Zaid You're very clever, you know lots of things.

Callum Thanks. My mum says I like facts.

Zaid I followed you in here because I've seen you at school
and I thought we should be friends.

Callum swings the knife like a samurai.
*Zaid finds this very funny. Callum is very pleased to
have made Zaid laugh.*

Callum That's my impression of a samurai.

Zaid That was really good.
What shall we do now?

Callum I don't know.
You're kind of naughty aren't you.

Zaid That's not very nice.

Callum Sorry. I mean . . . Sorry.

Zaid That's okay. What do you want to do now?

Callum I wonder what it feels like against our skin?

Zaid What do you mean?

Callum I wonder what the knife feels like against our skin.

Zaid We could try?

Callum Okay.

Callum puts the flat of the blade against his arm.

It's cold.

Zaid Wow. Cool.

Callum Yeah. It feels really cool actually. Do you want to try?

Zaid Yeah.

Callum holds out the knife.

Do it for me.

Callum Huh?

Zaid Yeah hold it against my arm for me.

Zaid holds his arm out, wrist up. Callum puts the knife down on Zaid's forearm.

Wow. Feels like glass.

Callum This one time me and my brother were playing football and we smashed a window in the kitchen and then I picked up a bit of the glass and I put it in my mouth and it felt kind of cold but then my mum saw me and she was SO SO angry she screamed she was like SPIT IT OUT SPIT IT OUT and so I did.

Zaid That's funny. The way you said 'spit it out' like you were your mum. That was really funny. You're good at impressions.

Callum What's impressions?

Zaid I don't really know but you're good at them.

Callum smiles.

Callum Thanks.

Zaid You're really funny.

Callum puts the knife against his leg.

Callum Wow. That feels cool too.

He puts it on the back of his neck and then on the side of his face.
Zaid lifts up his T-shirt.

Zaid Do you want to put it on my tummy?

Callum Yeah that would be so fun.

Zaid Do it.

Callum puts the knife on Zaid's belly.

WOW.

Callum What's it like?

Zaid So so cold.

Callum Wow. That feels so cool.

Zaid Yeah.
You can take it off now.

He does.

What shall we do?

Callum Do you want to see my willy?

Zaid Erm –

Callum pulls his trousers and pants down.
And stands there with the knife in his hand.

,

Callum My brother told me they'll have hair on them one day.

Zaid What like on our heads?

Callum Yeah.

Zaid Wow. I hope your brother's wrong.

Callum Same.
Wonder if it . . .

Callum puts the knife against his penis.

Zaid Wow. What's it . . .

Callum Really. Really. Cold.
Do you want to try?

Zaid pulls his pants and trousers down.
Callum holds the knife out and moves to touch it against Zaid's penis . . .
Suddenly, the door swings open. Callum hides the knife behind his back.
Billy Bonkers, a children's entertainer in full costume, enters.
He looks at the boys. Zaid pulls his trousers up. Callum just stands there.

(*Whisper to Zaid.*) It's Billy Bonkers.

Zaid (*whisper*) I know it's Billy Bonkers I'm not an idiot.

B. Bonkers Well. What have we here?

Zaid Nothing.

B. Bonkers Doesn't look like nothing.

Zaid We were just . . .

B. Bonkers Just . . .?

Zaid Just playing.

B. Bonkers Oh yeah?

Callum We weren't doing anything we / were

Zaid (*whisper*) Put your trousers on

> *Callum realises his trousers are still down. He pulls them back up. As he does so, he manages to secretly drop the knife in the bin.*

Callum was just telling me about tigers.

Callum And then we / were

Zaid Shussh.

B. Bonkers You missed me putting all the presents in the birthday boy's arms.

Callum I like that bit.

B. Bonkers He held on to ten presents.

Zaid (*to Callum*) Let's go.

> *Zaid takes Callum's hand and walks him towards the door.*

B. Bonkers Were you doing something naughty in here boys?

> *The boys stop, still holding hands.*

Hmmm?

Zaid No.

B. Bonkers Other boys' bodies aren't to be played with.

Zaid Can we go now?

Callum (*to Zaid*) Do you think Billy Bonkers does wees?

Zaid (*ignoring him*) Can we go now please?

B. Bonkers So long as you agree to keep yourselves to yourselves.
Hmmm?

The boys nod.

Good. Off you go then. Cake time.

The boys leave.
   Billy Bonkers walks into a cubicle. As he shuts the cubicle-door behind him, the front door swings open. Jesse and Ali enter. They are a little older than Zaid and Callum.

Jesse We don't want to be too early that's why it's perfect to be in here for a bit –

Ali Yeah I heard that being like half an hour late is the best way of doing it

Jesse Definitely definitely.

Ali goes to piss in a urinal. He does not lower his pants and trousers to his ankles. Jesse goes to the sink and starts taking things out of his bag and neatly laying them out: shirts, jeans, hair gel.

Ali Do you think the St Mary's girls will be here?

Jesse Course they will. They wouldn't miss something like this are you kidding? The St Mary's one only goes until eight p.m. which is SO LAME

Ali Oh my God that is SO SO LAME.

Jesse Plus I heard the parents like stay in the gym? Like they have this upstairs gallery bit and the parents all go up there and like watch so they can like see their kids getting numbers and stuff it's actually so weird

Ali Oh my God I would like kill my mum if she did that

Jesse (*an attempt at a 'your mum' joke*) Yeah your mum!

Ali (*genuinely confused*) What?

Jesse Nothing.

Jesse goes to the clothes.

Okay. So. Whose is whose?

Ali The ripped jeans are mine and the blue shirt as well

Jesse No the ripped jeans are mine

Ali No they aren't I stole them off my brother remember?

Jesse Yeah you stole them off your brother for me

Ali Really?

Jesse Really.
You can have the blue shirt.

Ali Fine.

*Ali takes his top and trousers off so he is just in his pants.
Jesse stares at him.*

What?

Jesse Are you gay or something?

Ali No.

Jesse Why would you take your shirt AND trousers off at the same time?

Ali Quicker.

Jesse Obviously you take off your T-shirt, put on the new shirt, then you take off the trousers and put on the new trousers. Weirdo.

*Jesse takes his pile of clothes and goes into a cubicle.
Ali is stood there in his pants feeling a fool. He picks his clothes up and takes them into another cubicle.*

Ali (*from inside*) Those ripped jeans were supposed to be for me.

Jesse (*from inside*) Why don't you just rip the ones you've got?

Ali My mum got them for me last week.

Jesse So?

Ali Yeah that's actually a good point.

The sound of Ali ripping his jeans.

Jesse This is going to be crazy Ali.

Ali I know.

Jesse Who do you think will get the most numbers?

Ali Probably Charlie.

Jesse Damn. Yeah you're right.

Ali But you maybe second most.

Jesse Thanks.
You as well.

As they are talking, Simon comes in. He is dressed in a very well realised James Bond costume.
Dinner suit and bow tie. Hair slicked. He looks very sweet.
He hears the other two talking in the cubicle and excitedly gets into position. He pulls out a plastic gun and points it at the cubicles. He waits and waits as they talk.

Ali Yeah, thanks.

Jesse Shirt tucked in or out?

Ali Out, definitely out.

Jesse Yeah. In is for school. Out is for the disco.

Ali Exactly.

Jesse How many buttons undone do you think?

Ali Two. My mum said two.

Jesse Oh my God you're so gay who cares what your mum says.

Ali Yeah fair.

Jesse Right come on, let's do our hair.

They both come out of their cubicles, Ali has ripped his jeans in a way that only a boy on the verge of puberty could. Jesse's clothes are way too big for him.
As they come out, Simon steps forward and BOOMS in his very best voice:

Simon THE NAME'S BOND. JAMES BOND.

Simon is very, very proud of himself.
Jesse and Ali stare at him, processing what they are seeing . . .
And burst into hysterical laughter.
They laugh long and hard, maybe one of them rolls on the floor. Simon increasingly deflated as they do so.

What?? WHAT?
Shut up it was a joke.
Stop it.
OH MY GOD WHAT?

Jesse (*turning to Ali and pointing a finger gun at him*) The name's Bond.

Ali Gay Bond.

Jesse fake shoots Ali and he falls to the floor.
They laugh even more.

Simon Well what are you even dressed as? You look like my brother.

Ali Oh my God –

Jesse We're not dressed as anything

Simon Why not?

Jesse Oh I don't know, why aren't we dressed as anything Ali?

Ali Erm. Maybe because we're not eight years old Jesse.

Jesse CORRECT!

Simon It's a fancy-dress disco

Jesse / Oh my God.

Ali Simon everybody knows that it's only the year fives who actually come wearing fancy dress. Nobody actually plays by those rules.

Simon Oh / no.

Jesse You, my friend, are going to look like a total idiot

Simon Oh God this is going to be worse than my brother's bar mitzvah.

Jesse Nothing can be as bad as your brother's bar mitzvah.

Simon Do you think I have time to go home?

Jesse No way.
Okay guys. Come on. Here we go.

They all turn to the mirror and inspect themselves. Perfecting hair. Choosing how many buttons to do up etc.

Ali Our first proper disco.

Jesse Actually my second.

Simon Being in the car when your mum picked up your brother from last year's doesn't count Jesse.

Jesse . . . Erm he brought me back three J2os from the drinks table and I drank all of them that night. I think that counts.

Simon That's so dumb.

Jesse At least I'm not dressed as James Bond.

Ali That is a good point.

Simon Yeah. Fair. That is a good point.

Ali So. There's going to be St Mary's girls. And Fairhill girls. And maybe even St Christopher's girls.

Simon Oh my God.

Jesse Sick.

Ali Everyone remember their numbers?

Jesse Oh-seven-six-four-six two-eight-eight nine-five-seven

Ali Oh-seven-eight-six-eight nine-eight-eight one-two-four

Simon Oh-two-oh-seven five-six-seven nine-three-nine-three

They both look at him.

What?

Jesse A landline?

Simon Mum still won't let me have a phone.

Ali Fuck

Jesse I'm so glad I'm not you Simon.

Simon Yeah me too . . . I mean yeah . . . as in if I wasn't me I'd be glad I wasn't me . . . Yeah. Thanks.

Jesse I'm going to get the most numbers anybody has ever got.

Ali Johnny Taylor from two years above got thirty-seven once.

Simon That's a lie

Ali No it's not my brother said

Jesse I'm going to get thirty-eight. And you, Simon, are going to get none.

Suddenly, Charlotte and Lola, girls of a similar age dressed up in a very half-hearted way as fairies, walk in.
They freeze. The boys look at them. They look at the boys.
Suddenly everyone starts screaming.
They look at each other and scream for a weirdly long time. Then they stop.

Charlotte Sorry.

Lola We thought that . . .

Charlotte Sorry.

,

Jesse The . . . The . . .
  The girls' . . . yeah . . .

Simon The girls' toilet is the next one along.

Charlotte Thank you.

Lola Thanks.

Jesse Idiots.

Lola What?

Jesse Says it on the door.

Charlotte Erm . . . Yeah. Sorry.

They turn to leave.

Simon Hey wait.

They stop.
Simon takes a deep breath and steps forward.

Can I have your number?

Charlotte Sorry I don't have a phone . . .

Simon What about you?

Lola Ummm.

Simon Please.

Charlotte (*to Lola*) Let's go.

Simon Give me your number then you can go.

Lola What?

Simon If you give me your number then you can go.

Charlotte (*to Lola*) Do it.

Lola Do you have a . . .?

Simon I'll remember it.

Lola Oh-seven-six-five-eight

Simon Oh-seven-six-five-eight

Lola Two-six-eight

Simon Two-six-eight

Lola Oh-nine-four

Simon Oh-nine-four
Nice. Maybe I'll call you. Maybe not.

Lola Can we go now?

Jesse Whatever.

The girls turn and leave.

Simon Wow . . .

Ali That was . . .

Simon Wow . . .

Ali That. Was. Amazing.

Simon Oh my God.

Ali Wow.

Jesse Shame they were so ugly.

Simon Yeah.

Jesse Shall we go inside? We're half an hour late, which is perfect.

Jesse and Ali head to the door.

Simon I think I'm gonna . . .

Jesse Make yourself look a bit less James Bond-y?

Simon Yeah.

Jesse leaves.
    Ali turns back to Simon.

Ali Hey Si?

Simon Yeah?

Ali That was awesome man.

Simon Thanks.

Ali leaves.
    Simon exhales a huge lump of tension, looks at himself in the mirror.
    Three teenage boys, Jack, Hamza and Fred, enter.
    They are dressed in school uniforms, adapted to look as raggedy as possible.
    They can't see Simon but Simon can see them.

Jack Double maths can bend over and fist itself until it bleeds all over that fucking uber-paedo-neek and he drowns in his own juices I am NOT sitting through that again, I am NOT.

Hamza I'm messaging the others –

*The three of them find places to sit: on a sink, up against
a wall, on a window ledge etc. Maybe one of them pisses
in a urinal.*

Simon approaches Jack, fascinated by the shape of him.

Fred You sure no one saw us?

Jack Can you chill the fuck out?

*Simon looks at Fred, examining his clothes. Maybe he
strikes a pose in imitation.*

Hamza Man no one gives a shit it's basically not against
the rules.

Fred I mean it's definitely against the rules.

Jack You texted the others yeah?

*Simon untucks his shirt, modelling himself after these
older boys.*

Hamza Yeah.

Jack Sick. Pretty sure Oscar has fags.

Simon looks in the mirror. Ruffles his hair. And exits.

Fred I get caught skipping again I am actually so fucked

Jack The only thing that is fucked, Fred-Fred, is your mum.
When I fuck her.

Fred Great. That's great. Truly, you're a wordsmith Jack.

Jack And you're a neek, Fred.

Fred Do you know what I'm excited for Jack? For the day
when I walk into a bar with a ridiculously fit woman and
I sit down and I turn around to the waiter to order
a cocktail and it's you. Serving me. And I go: Oh hello. Jack
isn't it? Or was it James? Yes I remember you, you were
that little potato-headed cunt who used to call me a neek.
Could you get me the most expensive drink on the menu?

Jack The fit woman you're with?

Fred Yeah

Jack Is that your mum?

Hamza and Jack burst out laughing.

Fred It's beneath me, it's literally beneath me to dignify that with a response.

Jack Listen to this one I heard the other day. Why's it so good fucking twenty-one-year-olds?
There are twenty of them.

Hamza That's sick.

From off, we hear Oscar. Midway through this speech, he piles in, followed by Owen.

Oscar I can't take it any more man! She's too fit she's just TOO fit she shouldn't be allowed to teach history she's like an actual genuine fitty like not just school fit but like real world fit and she's sitting there talking to me about the Tudors and I'm sorry but I just have to I just have to –

Oscar runs straight into one of the cubicles, slams the door and locks it.

Owen You're an actual caveman.

Jack Fucking finally

Hamza We thought you were bailing

Owen throws a backpack down and finds a seat.

Owen Not bailing bro, just couldn't get through the doorway with this guy's hard-on it's actually rank.

Oscar (*from inside*) It's not rank it's natural!

Jack Have you been in Hargreaves?

Owen The one and only

Jack Fuuuuuuuuuckkkkkk

Fred To be fair she is mad fit

Hamza It's absurd

Fred And she's a great teacher

Owen Yeah I think that's what drives Oscar mad, her ability to translate the AQA learning goals into exciting exercises

Jack So. Come on. Let's do it.
Whose house?

,

Come on. Don't do this.

Owen Do what?

Jack Owen you literally said / that

Owen I did not literally say anything

Hamza I mean you definitely said / that

Fred Yeah I mean you did say –

Owen I didn't say shit. I said MAYBE. Maybe they'd be away. But they aren't so we can't.

Fred Fuck.

Jack Fuck are you serious right now? I've told like so many people

Owen Okay well you definitely shouldn't have done that so / whose

Jack You definitely shouldn't have lied about having a free yard

Owen I didn't lie I just / didn't

Fred Yeah he didn't lie

Oscar I think he / lied

Fred That's not really the point

Hamza / True.

Jack The point is that we don't have anywhere to do it and I refuse I flat out refuse to drink tinnies on the green and freeze my nuts off watching Fred trying to get with Annie Fletcher again.

This gets a very good response, which Jack is thrilled about.

Fred Trying?! Are you joking. Erm. Who fingered Annie Fletcher twice in one night at Hamza's? Hold on let me just check . . . Yes that's right that'd be me.

Jack You sure that wasn't your dick?

Everyone's a bit confused.

But then you like . . . said it was a finger . . . like after. So like . . . Because it's so small you were like 'yeah that was actually my finger' . . . because you've got such a small cock.

Everyone starts laughing at Jack's attempt at a joke.

FUCK OFFFFF

The laughter dies down.

Hamza But we are fucked. To be fair.

Fred Yeah we are fucked

Hamza man when will we be able to get into pubs it's sooooo long.

Jack Speak for yourself I get into pubs the whole time.

Owen Bullshit

Jack The New Inn is basically my regular

Owen You chat shit

Fred 'My regular' what a prick

Jack I mean I literally know the name of the woman behind the bar so . . .

Hamza (*an impression*) Hello could I have two Ribenas and a packet of salt and vinegar please.

Big laugh.

Owen Oi listen to this one. What do you call a fat girl with a rape whistle?
Optimistic.

The chain flushing in the cubicle. Oscar comes out. Looking very pleased with himself.

Oscar Now that, boys, feels a fuck of a lot better.

Fred You're repulsive. You're actually repulsive.

Owen They should lock you up mate.

Oscar Bunch of fucking Catholics over here. Better out than in, I say.

Fred It's not a shit, Oscar. You can say that about a shit, but your come is not the same as your shit.

Oscar My balls need emptying.

This makes everyone laugh a lot.

Jack (*an impression*) I Oscar and I need balls emptying

Fred I'm ashamed that you are a part of my life.

Hamza She is fit though

Jack Yeah to be fair she is mad fit

An impression.

Tell me about the poor laws Mrs Hargreaves, I want to know everything there is to know about Pitt the Younger because he was a very VERY bad boy wasn't he?

Hamza joins in.

Hamza (*an impression*) Fuck me like one of your six wives and I'll turn you into a protestant Daddy.

Laughter. Oscar has a go:

Oscar Me and my fellow Vikings have sacked this village and now we will pillage your women. You first Hargreaves!

Jack Ha! Yeah I'm gonna tie you to a stake and fuck you like a witch!

,

,

Oscar (*to Owen*) So are we doing this at yours or not?

Owen We are not

Jack Where are we gonna do it then?

Everyone looks at Jack.

No. No we can't we absolutely can't.

Fred Argh you fucking Jew, why not?

Jack Because of my weird stepdad

Fred Fuck that

Oscar Aren't stepdads supposed to be like . . . trying to win your affection and stuff?

Jack I mean I guess we could. But we'd have to go upstairs when they got back.

Hamza I could deal with that

Jack And we'd have to be like so so quiet. And no smoking once they got back. And no vomming inside either.
But yeah. I mean if we have ABSOLUTELY no other options then I suppose it could be possible.

Fred Oh fuck. Actually. Wait.

Jack What?

Fred There's an issue with yours.

Jack Why?

Fred It'll be pretty awkward

Jack Why would it be awkward?

Fred Because I didn't call back?

Jack What are you talking about?

Fred After I fucked your mum last night

> *This gets a huge response.*
>   *Jack sits there going bright red. The laughing isn't stopping. He stands and goes up to Fred.*

Jack I'm fucking sick of you man

Fred Oh big man what you gonna do?

Jack Fuck you up

Fred (*an impression*) Fuck you up.
    Why do you speak like that Jack you're literally from Hendon.

> *Jack launches a big punch at Fred's upper arm. It's hard and strange.*

Fred What the fuck man

Jack Just fuck off yeah

Fred You fucking spaz what are you doing?

Jack Don't call me a spaz and don't talk about my mum or I'll do it again

Fred Well don't BE a fucking spaz and then we won't call you a fucking spaz you fucking spaz

Jack throws another punch. Fred grabs Jack's hair. It's all quite strange and undignified.

Jack Get off my fucking hair you pussy what the fuck

Owen Can you stop we're trying to sort a night out here

The boys break apart.
Jack is hot with anger, tears in his eyes.

Jack My fucking hair what the fuck? If you're going to fight me punch me.

Fred I don't want to fight you Jack, Jesus

Jack I'm sick of your shit

Fred You need anger management mate

Oscar Okay can we just . . . Chill.

Owen Alright what about this one: I called the rape advice line the other night. Turns out, it's just for victims.

Jack has retreated to a corner.

Jack Oi Oscar you got fags?

Fred We are not smoking in here.

Jack You might not be, but I am
Oscar?

Oscar In my bag.

Jack goes to Oscar's bag and gets cigarettes out.

So. Where we doing it?

Owen We're going Jack's.

Hamza Are we Jack?

Jack Yeah course

Jack has clambered up onto a surface and cracked open a tiny window somewhere up high.
He goes to light a cigarette.

Fred Do you know how much trouble we'll get in if someone comes in?

Jack holds eye contact with Fred, and lights the cigarette.

Jack First one of the day's always the best innit?

Fred This is the kind of shit that could fuck my UCAS

Jack Ha! UCAS what a prick.
And I'm not from Hendon. I'm from Edgware.

Fred Fucking hell.

Fred stands up.

I'm going. I will bring a bottle of Glen's. Hyped boys, very hyped.

Oscar Yeah might come too

Jack For real?

Hamza Oi if he asks where I am say I'm at the nurse yeah?

Owen Yeah wait up I'm coming

Jack You as well? Come on we've basically done the whole lesson.
What about this one. What's the difference between your dead baby sister and the last pope?

Fred The last pope died a virgin.

Oscar So old.

Owen Later.

They leave. Hamza and Jack alone.

,

Hamza I swear you were from Hendon –

Jack Shush.

,

Jack stubs the cigarette out.

,

,

Jack punches the wall. It hurts his hand.

,

,

I really can't have people round to mine this weekend man.
    My mum would . . .

Hamza Yeah. Thought so.

Jack Fuck. How am I gonna . . .
    Fuck.

,

Hamza You got deodorant? Reeks of cig.

Jack Bag.

Hamza goes to Jack's bag and takes a can of deodorant.

Can't believe he's trying to get with Annie Fletcher.
    I mean Annie? Of all people. It's like he's trying to ruin
my life. She was my first, man. And that means something.
    That night was . . .
    Man that night was magical. We were on her bed. And
I'm wasted. Remember when the guy on the corner would
only sell us White Lightning?

Hamza You've told me before / man

Jack We're lying next to each other on this big pink bed
she's got and we're getting with each other.

Hamza starts spraying the deodorant.
    *He keeps his finger down on the button and walks
around the room.*

But I'm so gone, you know, I'm kind of zoning in and out?
Kind of like pressing fast forward and then hitting play for
a bit. And when I do come to, I think WOW. I'm fucking
Annie Fletcher right now. And then it fast forwards again
and I open my eyes and it's like . . . yeap. I'm actually losing
my V to Annie Fletcher this is crazy.

And there's this moment right, kind of towards the end
when I look at her and her eyes are sort of rolled back? But
it's weird because it's not like porn eyes rolled back it's kind
of like . . . demented? Like not fit at all.

Hamza stops spraying. Looks at Jack.

And then I finished.

I finish and she goes to the toilet.

Hamza My sister said they always do that after. To like get
the come out? Or it like fucks them up or something.

Jack Rank what does your sister know?

Hamza Nothing man I just . . .

Jack Anyway it's different holes

Hamza What?

Jack For your dick and for their piss. It's two different
holes.

Hamza Bullshit.

Jack It is.

Hamza How is that even possible?

Jack I don't know man.

Just is. Anyway, she comes back and then she lies down
and falls asleep next to me. And then I need a piss too so
I go into the toilet which is attached to her room. I mean
she's minted you should have seen this crib. But I go in
there and there's like . . . vom everywhere?

41

Hamza What?

Jack Vomit on the floor and in the toilet and even like up the wall

So I piss, watching not to get my feet in any of it or anything like that – and then I go back into the room and she's still asleep. And I look at her lips. And they're parted a little bit. And I'm just staring at her lips –

Hamza But she's got a vommy mouth –

Jack I've been dreaming of her lips for years man. For years and years you know. For like . . . fuck man I had my first successful wank over her. Like the first time I ever came, where something actually came out, I was thinking about her mouth . . . And there it was.

Hamza So what did you do?

Jack I'm still sort of hard you know? And like she had been so up for it. You know proper gagging for it. So she gave me head.

And I came in her mouth.

Like a fucking come-shot man it was absurd

Hamza My God.

Jack And second time around it takes longer you know? To come. So it was proper stuff. Proper good. Kind of like face-fucking? You ever seen that?

Hamza Then what happened?

Jack Well. I don't know. My come was on her mouth. And by then I was soft and I couldn't stop thinking about the vom.

Hamza Right yeah the vom.

Jack So I just left.

Her sister was there when I came down the stairs.

Hamza Was she fit?

Jack She had a dressing gown on and was holding a hot water bottle. Think she might have had swimming goggles round her neck?

Hamza Swimming goggles?

Jack Yeah maybe she'd been like chopping onions or something.

Hamza Right. Yeah my mum does that sometimes.

Jack Got the night bus home.
It was so special man. That whole night. It was like magic.
Fucking Fred man.

,

Hamza starts spraying the deodorant again.

,

,

,

,

,

,

,

,

,

,

Eventually:
The spray can runs out.
Hamza shakes it and sprays a bit of deodorant under each armpit.

,

43

Hamza Heard this one the other day:
It's not rape if she's a dead bear and I just lost my job at the circus.

,

Yeah I don't really get it to be honest.

From off, we hear the voice of an angry-sounding teacher:

Mr Thomas Oi. Is anyone in here?
Hello?

The boys freeze.
We hear the teacher walking around, knocking on different doors, all the while getting closer and closer.

I know you're in one of them. You might as well own up now.

Hamza (*whispers*) What do we do?

Jack He's not allowed to come in.

Hamza Course he can come / in

Jack He can't it's some paedo law.

Mr Thomas Hello?
Boys. Is anybody in there?
Come on. I know you're skiving. Out. Now.

Hamza Get in the cubicle

Jack Fuck off are you joking???

Hamza Fuck this I'm so fucked.

Mr Thomas You'll be in less trouble if you just come forward now

He's right up by the door now. He knocks on it a few times.

Jack My mum is going to murder me.

Mr Thomas I am going to come in there. I can hear you. You must think I'm a fucking idiot. I'm coming in there in five.

Four.

Three.

Hamza jumps up onto the ledge and somehow manages to crawl through the high-up window. It's as though he's disappeared in the blink of an eye.

Two.

Jack finds himself standing there, alone.
He looks at the door. He looks at the window.

One!

The door swings open revealing not Mr Thomas, but Ace, an older (masked) boy with his hood up.

Ace (*calling back behind him*) Yo come this one's free!

Jack What the . . .

Ace White fucking walls

Jack Who are . . .

Ace opens the door back up and shouts out:

Ace Come on let's go!!!!!!

Jack, in disbelief, slowly backs into a cubicle and closes the door behind him.

(*To himself.*) Perfect.

Ace takes a spray can out from somewhere. He moves like a wild animal.

Hurry up man!!!!

He looks up at a wall, contemplating what to write.
Jay comes in. He's dizzy with adrenaline, twitchy as anything.

Jay Fuck this man fuck this fuck this

Ace Last one come on

Jay Come on man I'm done with this shit I'm done let's go

Ace has started graffitiing the toilet.

LET'S GO HE'S COMING MAN
    Fuck. FUCK FUCK FUCK. I shouldn't have fucking come I shouldn't have fucking –

Jay opens the door and leans out.

Ace What shall we write

Jay He saw us do the last one there's fucking police I can't get a record man I can't

Ace It's graffiti Jay it's not murder

Jay My dad will kill me man he'll actually kill me
    They're coming they're fucking coming over here I swear FUCK

Jay tries to pull Ace away.

Ace Get the fuck off me alright?

Ace pushes him away.

Jay I'm trying to help you.

Ace I don't want your help.
    I said GET OFF ME.

> *From outside we hear the sound of a fight breaking out. The voices are muffled, but they are loud and aggressive-sounding. Genuinely threatening.*
>
> **Liam** (*from off*) I'll put you in a fucking coma that's what I'll do you little cunt

Jo (*from off*) Oi get the FUCK off me yeah?

A smashing sound.

Jay I'm running

Ace Yeah fucking course you are you're always running you said you were up for it but you're running

Jay You're going too far that's your problem you always go too far.

Jay turns and runs out. Ace stands there, spray can in hand. He's managed to cover much of the bathroom in graffiti but a big patch of white wall is left, which he looks up at.

Another smash.

Liam (*from off*) Oh fucking big man?

Jo (*from off*) Get off me I'll –

Liam (*from off*) You'll fucking what?

Ace stands there, leg pumping, thinking about what to write.

Ace starts to spray something.

Another crash from off, much nearer this time. The sound of some heavy bass from a big sound system begins to creep in through the walls. It's quiet at first, but it slowly ramps up as

Ace keeps spraying.

the sound of the fight gets nearer and nearer.

(*From off.*) Look at you, you look like a fucking clown. You're a fucking clown aren't you? You're a stupid fucking clown is what you are.

SMASH.

The sound of the music and the fight growing louder and louder.

The music grows.

SMASH.

Ace has finished his work. He stands back and takes a moment to look at it. In its own way, it is beautifully drawn.

Suddenly, from off, Jo is punched into the room. He slams into a wall. He is bloody.

Liam follows, picks him up and throws him into a cubicle, which he smashes through.

Ace has one more look at his work, turns on his feet and flees.

Liam is now kicking the shit out of Jo.
   The music has died down a little, as though coming from a room next door.

48

Liam I warned you! I fucking warned you!

Liam stops. He stands over Jo, fist raised.

You're a lucky little boy. You know that?
Look at you. Fucking . . .
Shit man.

Liam turns and runs out the room. As he opens the door the music gets louder, and then quieter again as it closes.

Movement Two

Jo is sat there, slumped.

,

He has blood coming from somewhere on his head. We sit with him a while as he drops in and out of consciousness.

From outside we hear the music come to an end. The sound of a big crowd cheering.

Something muffled is shouted through a microphone. Another cheer.

And then we hear the start of a new DJ set. Over the entirety of this Movement, we hear the rise and fall of the set. It's heavy, techno-y. Joyful at times, industrial at others.

Jo looks around the room, trying to get his bearings. He puts his hand to his head and looks at it. Blood.

He tries to get to his feet, but this proves difficult.

Eventually, he's up. The door swings open and two guys come in: Dee and Cal.

Jo goes over to a urinal in the corner and shields himself from them, pretending to piss.

Cal Beautiful it was actually beautiful.

Cal goes to piss at a urinal. Dee stands at the sinks waiting for him.

Dee Can't believe she dropped that in the middle of it

Cal Such a flex

Dee SUCH a flex.
It was so . . .

Cal Beautiful. Actually beautiful. The way she . . . . URGH she's an actual God it's INSANE

Dee Nuts man

Cal Even better than last time I think

Dee For sure

Cal Crazy good vibes

Dee Such a good crew man

Cal finishes and heads to the sinks. He washes his hands.
So happy you're here man.

Cal Thanks man. So happy to be here. It's been too long.

Dee Yeah man.

They hug. It's nice.

Cal Ready for the next?

Dee I was born ready baby.

They head to the door.

Cal Drink?

Dee OH MY GOD that is EXACTLY / what I . . .

They're gone.
Jo turns around. He goes to the mirror. He is a little shocked by his appearance. The door swings open and Milo comes in. He's wearing very little.
They stop and look at each other.

Milo Wow.
Fuck.

Jo Costume.

Jo ducks into a cubicle.
Milo goes to the mirrors. He turns a tap on and splashes his face. He's coming up on drugs and trying to keep himself level.
Some time goes past as he breathes deeply and holds on to the sink.

Milo It's a good costume man.
   Really good.
   Had me, for sure.
   Wow I need a sit down.

Milo goes into a cubicle. He sits down on the toilet, keeping the door open so we can see him.

It's always the second one that does you in isn't it?

He puts his head between his legs and breathes deeply for some time.

   Eventually Milo starts to move a little to the music. He seems to grow in stature as he moves, recovering from his wobble.

You know what mate? I think I might have just gone and turned the corner. Oh yes sir. Milo has turned a corner.

He jumps to his feet, a spring in his step and a smile on his face.

Ah. I do need a shit though.

Pulls his trousers down, sits and starts having a shit, keeping the door open.

Sick costume man. Really.
   Yo.

Jo Thanks.

Milo Yes mate. Pretty gnarly. You know when I came in I was struggling a bit there, it was all spinning and nauseous you know? And then I saw you and it was like some terrible trip or something. You gotta be careful with that kind of costume you know?

Jo Yeah. But I'm fine.

Milo Yeah. I know. I mean why wouldn't you be?

Jo Exactly.

Milo Good night?
  Mine's been great. This guy's sick.

Terry, a man in a gigantic peacock costume, walks in. He walks to the urinal and pisses. He finishes, looks at himself in the mirror. Fluffs his feathers. Nods to Milo. Exits.

Wow.
  Crazy night man.
  Still got hours to go too. Always nice when you check the time and it's earlier than you thought.

Milo finishes. He stands up, flushes the chain and goes to the sink where he washes his hands.

Well that's me done.

He waits for an answer.
  Nothing. He moves closer to Jo's cubicle. This image might remind us of the Father and Boy from the opening scene.

You sure you're alright in there mate?

Jo What?

Milo Yeah all good man all good. Just saying you sure you're alright in there yeah?

Jo Yes mate.

Milo Cool cool. Sick costume yeah.

Jo Yes mate.

Milo Because you know if you did need any help with anything then you know I / could easily

Jo (*aggressive*) I'm alright mate just leave it yeah?

Milo Course cool yeah man.
  Well.

Milo leaves.
From inside Jo's cubicle we hear:

Jo Hello?
Yeah
Still here still here
yeah

*The cubicle door swings open and Jo comes out, playing
with his phone. He types something and holds it up to
his ear.*

Hello? Fuck's sake.

He does the same again.

Hey yeah I'm still here there was a fight my leg is . . . .
Hello?

He looks at the phone.

Yeah I'm here I said.
I'm dizzy I
Hello?

Suddenly he screams:

FUCK!!

*He throws the phone at a wall and it smashes. He sinks
to his knees and sobs.*
*Marty, a big and gentle man, walks in. He sees Jo
crouched there. Jo doesn't see him. Marty backs out of
the room.*
*Jo gathers himself. He goes to the mirror and starts to
inspect his wounds properly. A gash above his eye is
painful to touch.*
He lifts up his shirt to inspect his torso.
Marty walks back in and Jo pulls his shirt back down.

Marty Hi.

Jo Alright?

Marty pisses as Jo inspects his face, assessing the damage. Marty comes to the sink and washes his hands.

Marty Troublesome night?

Jo Huh?

Marty Looks like you've had a troublesome evening.

Jo No trouble mate.

Marty You've someone you can call?

Jo Costume, mate.

Marty Right.
Good to get a little break in the toilet, isn't it? Tag out. Have a little me time.
If that's your phone down there, then you can borrow mine. Maybe there's someone you'd like to call.

Jo looks at him.

You're not in trouble. I'm a doctor.
I should probably have a look at your . . .
I've been coming to this night for ten years love, I know a costume when I see one.
Can I?
It's alright friend. No trouble.

Jo nods.
Marty walks up to him. He's about to reach out to inspect his face when Sid, a man in shorts and nothing else, comes in.
Jo moves away from Marty as Sid comes in.

It's alright. You're alright.

Sid pisses. Hesitantly, Jo gives himself over to Marty a little.

Oh. Before I look. I do have a confession to make.

Jo What?

Marty I'm a nurse. Not a doctor.

Jo smiles. Marty smiles. It's nice.
Sid finishes his piss and leaves.
Marty talks as he inspects Jo.

I guess this face explains that cubicle huh?
Turn to the left. Does that hurt?

Jo makes a sound which suggests it does.

Try opening your mouth. A little wider. Okay. Good.
And follow my finger.
Good.
And again.
Good.
Can you hear this?

He brushes his fingers together beside one ear.

Jo Yes.

Marty And this?

,

Jo Uh-huh.

Marty What's your name friend?

Jo Alright mate that's enough yeah

Marty Don't worry you're okay. I'm a nurse, remember?

Jo Yeah.

Marty Well why don't we clear you up, get you looking the
part.

Jo Yeah, sure.

Marty Fighting. Waste of everyone's time, I say.

Marty goes to the toilet and takes some loo roll. He wets
it in the sink and goes about clearing up Jo's face.

Jo You been coming here for a while then?

Marty Oh yes, that's me. Old guard.
   First time?

Jo Yeah think so.

Marty These old bones of mine still find a way of moving on a dance floor. I can't explain it. Sleep in the wrong position and that's my back gone for a week. But drop a beat, and I'm like Tinker Bell.
   Looks like you've got some trouble on your torso there too.

Jo's face is clean now.

Jo Yeah hurts like fuck to be honest.

Marty Do you mind lifting your shirt up, let me have a quick look?
   Better to check. You might need help.

Jo I'm a bit . . . confused? I was here with my mates. I was dancing and then there was a guy with a beer? Like at the bar? I'm just a bit confused.

Marty I understand. You might be concussed. Best not to have anything else to drink tonight. Do you mind if I . . . ?

Jo nods.
   Marty lifts up his shirt.

Oof. He gave you a good going over didn't he?
   I'm going to touch your body a little bit now. Is that okay?

Jo nods.

I'm sorry if my hands are cold. Dancing always does that to me. Funny that, isn't it?

Marty places a hand on some ribs.

Does this hurt?

57

Jo No.

Marty And this?

Jo No.

Marty Good. Do you mind turning around? Won't take
a second.

Jo turns around.

Where are you from then?

Jo Nearby.

Marty Nice. Nice around here. A little expensive these
days. I remember when it was all run-down flats and dodgy
shops. Mind you, I didn't have some half bad nights in
those flats. Does that hurt?

Jo A little.

Marty Probably best to have someone accompany you
home tonight.
      Any pain there?

Jo No.

Marty And what did you say your name was again friend?
      Don't worry, it's not a test.

Jo What are you doing?

Marty I'm just checking you're alright.

*Marty moves his hands up onto Jo's shoulders and starts
to move down his collar bones.*

How's that?
      And that.
      How about that?

Jo Can you get off me yeah?

Marty Excuse me?

Jo Who the fuck are you can you get the fuck off me?

Marty I'm just checking you haven't –

Jo spins around and catches Marty in the face as he does so. Patrick, tie-dye T-shirt and bucket hat, walks in and goes to a urinal.

Jo I said get off me yeah I'm fine.

Marty I was just . . .

Jo You were just what?

Marty Just checking you were okay.

Jo Didn't fucking feel like that mate, felt a little different to checking I'm alright.

Patrick looks up from his piss.

Patrick Everything alright?

Jo Yeah fine.

Patrick Only love boys.

He goes back to his piss.

Jo I'm fine, okay? Just fuck off would you.

Marty I don't know if you are fine.

Jo If I wanted help I would have asked for it.
Are you even a nurse? Bet you're not even a nurse.

,

Fucking hell –

Marty I'm training.

Jo Jesus. Training. Touching me up is what you're doing –

Marty That is absolutely not what / I was

Jo Get out.

Marty Calm down friend

Jo Get out or *you'll* go into a fucking cubicle.

Marty takes a look at him, sadly.

Marty He had a point. That bloke who smashed your head in.

Whatever you do, don't take anything else tonight.

Marty leaves.
Patrick finishes his piss, heads to the sink.

Patrick Peace man.

He puts a fist out to fist-bump Jo.
Jo just looks at it.

Peace.

Patrick leaves.
And all of a sudden,
Jo vomits into one of the sinks.
The door opens. Kay and Ollie come in. They are in the middle of an animated conversation. Through the following Jo just stands by the sink, swaying a little. Nodding in and out, maybe.

Kay So we make eye contact at like Vauxhall.

Ollie He remembers the station

Kay Of course he remembers the station this girl is like . . .

Ollie Is like . . .

Kay Absurd. She's absurd.

Ollie (*seeing Jo*) Oh hello what have we here.

Kay Someone's had a good one.

They go to piss at the urinals, ignoring Jo.

So anyway. I'm sat opposite her on the Victoria and she's unreal man she's got like tatts up her arm and fucking shaved side of the head and just fit as fuck. Like OH MY GOD the fucking shoes she was wearing? She's got style and grace and her lips I wanted to –

Ollie Rub your cock

Kay YES. Rub my cock and fucking put my head between her legs and have her piss in my mouth. I wanted her to piss on me and lick the inside of my mouth and FUCK I would do anything man. I mean she could peg me. She could actually peg me and I'd / be totally

Ollie Have you been pegged before?

Kay No man I haven't been fucking pegged. Anyway we're at Green Park and . . .
   Wait have you been pegged?

Ollie Once.

Kay Once.
   Wow. I mean once is enough innit. Been pegged once you've been pegged a thousand times. How was it.

Ollie Kind of mad.

Kay Anyway, we're at Highbury now and we sort of made eye contact but she's on the phone you know sort of listening or texting or some shit. You know how they do that sometimes? Anyway, we sort of make eye contact and I'm dying inside at this point you know? I'm going to blow up I'm imagining our future together. I'm meeting her mum and we're doing a wedding but a sort of unconventional one you know where everyone's on diz and the best man is wearing a dress and she's wearing a suit because she's like that you know?
   And then we're at Seven Sisters and I'm like okay okay there is definitely a thing here there is definitely some kind of vibe here there must be a vibe we are looking right into each other's eyes you know we're fucking each other in the eyeballs COME ON there is a full-blown-vibe and then all

of a sudden and without warning . . . she stands up from her seat and she leaves.

She just turns and she leaves and then I'm sat there and next thing I know I'm at Tottenham and I think I've missed the best thing that could have ever happened to me. The woman of my dreams. This whole alternative future. Which is bright and sunny and exciting and extreme and full of emotions and sensations and risks and fucking LIFE man full of all these things and it's GONE. It's fucking stood up and walked off the train because I didn't have the nuts to stand up and say: Hey. I'm Kay. I'm sound. I'm great, in fact. And we should have a drink and find out if my first instincts were correct. I think I love her.

Ollie Wow. You have the romantic sophistication of a teenage boy in a shit film

They start walking out.

Kay But I felt it man. I really felt it. It felt so real.

They're gone.
Jo stumbles backwards a bit, almost tripping up over himself. He looks up into the mirror.

Jo Where am I?

The door opens and two drag queens come in: Vanessa Feltz and Maureen Lip-Man.
Over the following, Jo looks over to them, smiling. Vanessa and Maureen try to ignore him, until they can't.

Maureen I'm absolutely gagging for a shit.

Vanessa In you go.

Maureen goes into a cubicle. Vanessa goes to a urinal.

Maureen It's completely rank in here.

Vanessa I like it

Maureen That's because you like terrible places.

Vanessa It's got character

Maureen It's got Hep-B on the seats is what it's got.

Vanessa For a terrible place you do love coming here every weekend

Maureen I come here because you bring me here babe

Vanessa Lies

Maureen And you only come here because you're exercising some kind of weird class guilt that makes you want to be in shit places rather than nice places.

Vanessa I'm exercising a love of techno

Maureen I hate techno. Nobody actually likes techno.

Vanessa That's too stupid a statement to dignify with a response

Maureen What's wrong with Soho House?

Vanessa Everything is wrong with Soho House

Maureen They know my name there and everyone has fantastic coke

Vanessa You're despicable. And basic as fuck –

Maureen OH MY FUCKING GOD there isn't any bog roll.

She walks like a crab out of her cubicle into the next one, which has toilet paper in it.

Vanessa Jesus Christ I didn't know Maureen Lip-Man did such terrible shits.

Maureen (*a Maureen Lipman BT advert impression*) He never calls! He never writes! He never smells my terrible shits!

Vanessa (*a Vanessa Feltz impression*) My boy comes round every week. But I suppose when you live in Totteridge, / the Beverly Hills of North London

Maureen The Beverly Hills of North London –

Vanessa It's a pleasure to come round to your grandmother's house.

Vanessa is doing her make-up in the mirror.

You know however hard I try to become Vanessa Feltz, I always end up looking a bit more Vanessa Kirby.

Maureen In your dreams.

Jo watches Vanessa, fascinated.

Vanessa Maureen?

Maureen Yeah.

Vanessa Vomit boy is watching me.

Maureen You've no one to blame but yourself. You bring us to putrid places, you get looked at by boys covered in their own sick.

The chain flushes. Maureen comes out and joins Vanessa. They both start touching up their make-up.

She really is looking isn't she?

Vanessa To be fair to her I don't know if she's totally conscious.

Maureen (*to Jo*) Oi. Take a fucking picture.

Jo My phone broke.

Vanessa Got you there. Pass that would you?

She passes some make-up.

Jo Looks great.

Maureen Where are the others?

Vanessa In the smaller room upstairs.

Maureen There's a second room?

Vanessa You won't like it.
  Strange crowd isn't it

Maureen Sweaty and po-faced. I find them deeply unappealing.

Jo is still staring.

Sorry babe can I help you?

Jo Just interested, you know?

Maureen Interested in what?

Jo What it feels like?

Vanessa What *what* feels like

Maureen A smack in the face?

Jo Always wondered what it feels like to put on lipstick, you know?

Maureen Fucking hell

Vanessa Leave it hun she's alright

Maureen He.

Jo You know I've just always wondered? Like what it would feel like on my mouth because my sister did it to me once and it was horrible and sort of sticky. I didn't like it you know?

Maureen Something sticky on your mouth, is that right?

Jo Yeah sort of suffocating you know?

Maureen (*to Vanessa*) I didn't come out to be harassed by some normie fuck-boy.

Vanessa Oh come on be nice.
  (*To Jo.*) Well maybe you should try it one day babe? You might find it liberating.

Maureen Ha! Typical.

Vanessa Why typical?

Maureen You and your conversion mission.

Vanessa (*to Jo*) I think you'd find it exciting.

Maureen Vanessa, the queer prophet, preaches the word of the Lord to all who have ears to listen.

Vanessa (*to Jo*) You can borrow some of mine if you want.

Maureen (*to Vanessa*) You should open a straight boys conversion therapy centre. Picking up drunk men in club toilets. They walk in dressed like a Peaky Blinder, listening to Oasis. They leave as Dolly Parton with a handbag full of anal beads.

Jo Maybe I will try it.

Maureen Don't worry hun. You just do you, huh?

Jo You see this one time when I was at school / I was

Maureen Here we go

Vanessa Be nice!

Jo Yeah it's just I wonder why you dress like that you know?

Maureen Excuse me?

Jo Yeah it's just this / one

Maureen Come on enough of this let's go

Vanessa Let me just finish this one sec

Jo I was at school and it was home clothes day and that. You know home clothes day? Sort of where you get to wear your own clothes? Like you don't need to wear all that itchy school uniform and stuff you could just stick on whatever you'd wear on a Saturday or a Sunday or –

Maureen We understand the concept of home clothes day –

Jo Yeah course. Yeah.
   You're beautiful.

Vanessa What?

Jo So it's a Friday morning and I'm staying at my stepdad's for whatever reason and I'm getting dressed into school uniform when I suddenly remember . . . FUCK. It's home clothes day. You know you don't want to be that kid on home clothes day who's forgotten. That kid's a fuckhead. And I was for sure not going to . . . Anyway I'm sleeping in my stepdad's kids' room. Or sort of like the room that his kids sleep in when they're with him you know. And he's got a daughter and a son, so I'm in their shared room with all their shit. There's like WWF posters but also fucking make-up or whatever –

Maureen (*to Vanessa*) Let's go

Vanessa Wait I want to hear the end of this

Maureen Are you serious?

Jo So I'm standing there in the kids' room and I open the cupboard and I'm like . . . okay. What have we got?
  I go through the T-shirts and they're all basically way too tight. I guess the kids must have been younger when they were living there or something but I try a few on and it's awful it's all like Action Man T-shirts that I'm basically popping out of and I've got a kind of belly too which I'm ashamed of you know I wish I could slice it off I look disgusting and these T-shirts are not doing me any favours. So I look and I look and I look and I'm getting pretty worked up. I'm at the house alone and I don't want to be late for school because things weren't going great for me at school at that moment either so / I'm sort of keen

Maureen Come on let's get the fuck out of here

Vanessa You go I'll see you by the bar

Maureen What? What is this doing for you? What part of you is this reaching?

Jo And then I find this shirt.

It's flowery? Kind of like paisley? It's really bright and it's kind of like nothing I've ever seen before let alone worn, and it's very different from the trackies and hoodies and that I've got back in my cupboard at home.

Maureen Are you actually going to sit through this?

Jo And I look at this shirt and I think. Okay. Well. Maybe I'm that person? You know maybe that's me?

Maureen I'm done. I'm actually done. I'm finding the others. Last chance.

Jo So I get my school trousers and I rip them a little so they look like home clothes and then I put on this shirt. And I turn around a few times in the mirror and it looks kind of weird? Like kind of gay you know?

Maureen Okay goodbye.

Maureen leaves.

Jo But I wear it and I stuff my uniform in my bag and I get on the bus. And I remember so clearly sitting on the bus you know. Like I knew nobody on it and they didn't know me and so it was like . . . WOW. You guys think this is me. You guys think I am the kind of guy who wears this shirt. And you know it felt like floating. It felt like being totally invisible. Like some kind of magic where I was undercover. But also sort of not undercover. Sort of the opposite of undercover? Argh I can't explain it but / anyway

Vanessa You're doing a good job of it

Jo I get off the bus and I see this alternative me open up before me you know. A different me and I think: well. This is me now. I wear flowery shirts and that's that. And I turn into the school gates and as I turn I see a teacher. He's this Biology teacher. I only sort of half knew him but not really. He was always smoking by the bins and a bunch of people thought he was a legend but I never really got it. Anyway

he sort of gave me this look? Like this sort of like 'Oh?'
I mean now I think about it maybe he was just nodding or
whatever but it looked to me like a look like 'Oh? Really?
You? In that shirt?' And he walked past and then I walked
into school with my head down and I walked straight to the
toilets and I took my school shirt back out of my bag and
took the flowery shirt off and buried it in the bottom of
a bin and then I spent the rest of the day pretending I was
the fuckhead who'd forgotten it was home clothes day.
     My head hurts. Man. Does your head hurt too? It's . . .

Jo holds his ear as though hearing a painful noise.

Does your head hurt?

Vanessa looks at him like he's a stray dog.
     *She puts her hand out and holds his cheek, very
tenderly.*
     *Hunter comes in, dressed in nothing particularly
striking. He goes into a cubicle.*

What's . . .
What's my name?

Vanessa It's okay. You're okay.

Jo But I can't remember my name.

Vanessa takes her hand off his cheek and exits.
     *Hunter comes out of the cubicle. He is now dressed in
an extraordinarily well realised demon costume. It is
genuinely terrifying. A different calibre of fancy dress
than we've seen thus far.*
     Wait . . . is that even a costume?

Hunter Now you, pal, are what I would call worse for wear.

Jo turns and is shocked by what he sees.

Jo Fucking hell . . . You're . . . Didn't see you . . .

Hunter (*calling out*) Come on mate. Gagging over here.

Frank emerges from another cubicle. He is also dressed in his own spin on the demon costume.

Frank (*to Hunter*) Absolutely crawling with fitties in there.

Jo spins around, stunned by Frank's presence.

Hunter Hold the door would you?

Hunter goes to a sink and pours some drugs out onto his phone. Jo can't quite understand what he's seeing.
Frank stands by the door, putting his foot in the way so no one can come in.

Jo Sorry do you mind if I leave . . .

Hunter You want in do you pal?

Jo No I . . . Where did you come from?

Frank Alright, alright. It's good to share, I suppose. Isn't that right Hunter?

Hunter That's right.

Jo Were you in there the whole time . . . ?

Hunter In where?

Jo Sorry could I leave please

Hunter Frank's just holding the door. You don't want anyone coming in when you're indulging you know? Can get in awful trouble.

Hunter does some drugs.

Jo Your costumes are . . .

Frank Thanks very much

Hunter We're Mephistopheles and Lucifer

Jo Right.

Frank You know who they are?

Jo My head hurts, I think I'm going to be sick?

70

Frank A pick-me-up is what you need pal

Hunter Come on. Not going to wait all day for you

   Hunter gestures to the drugs.

Do you want or not? I'm offering you free drugs mate. You mad?

Jo No I think I'll just leave.

Frank That won't be possible on account of me holding the door shut

Hunter Will you be having some or not?

   Jo goes to him.

Thata boy.

   Jo does lots of drugs.

Wow easy tiger

Jo I think I should go . . .
   Wait . . . what did you say those costumes were?

   A knock on the door.

Hunter That'll be the others. Let them in would you?

Frank Yeap.

   *Frank keeps his foot in front of the door.
      Instead, he clicks his fingers. Oz and Ola walk in
      through the walls. They too are dressed like demons.*

Ola Oi Oi!

Oz You billing up big boy?

Hunter Most certainly.

Ola Who's this?

Oz New mate?

Frank Straggler

Jo Who are you? Wait were you . . .

        Where did . . .

  My head . . . My fucking

                Head

  Can you not shine that light please?

Ola Ola

Oz And I'm Oz

Ola Wild in there innit

Oz Absolute madness. Let's have some of that

  Oz does some drugs. More knocking on the door.

Jo Your costumes are . . .

Hunter Thank you very much

Ola Good aren't they?

Oz Nothing like ketamine at this time of the night, is there?

Jo Who did you say you were?

Frank We're the Four Horsemen of the Apocalypse

Ola The ones whom the Lord hath sent to patrol the earth

Hunter Sword

Oz Famine

Frank Wild Beasts

Ola Plague

Hunter And together we shall bring forth the cataclysm of the apocalypse

Ola Or something like that

Oz Yeah something like that

Frank Where's that knife gotten to?

Ola Check the bin, Oz. Always good to check what's been buried at the bottom of a bin, isn't it Jo?

Oz plunges his hand into the bin, and pulls out the knife dropped by Callum in the first Movement. He starts playing with it.

Frank First comes the Antichrist.

Hunter Then comes War.

Oz Then comes Famine in a golden carriage.

Ola Then comes Death.

Jo Wait what . . . ketamine did you say?

Did you   did you

         say that was

Ket. Like

Oz Greedy boy wants more does he?

Jo No . . . I thought it was . . .
The room's spinning a bit

           isn't it.

               Could you . . .

I said

    Could you

       Could you STOP

            Could you STOP
            SHINING that light?

The DJ set is reaching a climax. It seems louder. Intense. The knocking on the door turns to banging. By now, Jo has pissed himself.

Hunter Yeah. I would say the room is definitely spinning.

Ola Wow nelly.

Oz Wow nelly indeed.

Frank sings the first few lines of 'Nellie the Elephant'.

Jo Who's the Four Horsemen of the Apocalypse?

Hunter There's no escaping who you are, Jo.

Jo Jo? Who's Jo? Am I Jo? How do you –

Oz Don't be pissing on yourself Jo. That's got to be rule number one. Do not piss on thine own self.

Ola That shirt'll make you look like a little queer, Jo

Oz There's no changing who you are, Joseph. You're not a good person Joseph. Another smack in the face will feel good won't it Joseph.

Frank I'm Beelzebub.

Oz I'm Mammon.

Ola Leviathan

Hunter Sathanas

Oz We're missing the other three. Perhaps you could help?

Ola has started punching a cubicle door over and over. He's thumping it hard.

Jo What's he doing?

Frank It's something he does sometimes.

Jo Why?

Hunter We don't really know. But it seems to be good for him. It seems to help him get something out. Best not to disturb him, we find.

Jo Doesn't it hurt?

Frank Not whilst he's doing it, no.

Jo is bleeding out of his ear by now.

Jo Did you

                 say

that was

                   ketamine?

Oz Maybe it'd be easier if we cut off our cocks. What do you say lads?

Oz goes over to Jo and holds the knife against his penis.

You don't mind if I . . . do you?

Oz pulls Jo's pants and trousers down. He stares at his penis.

Frank You've got something coming out of your ear mate.

Jo touches his ear and sees blood.

Oz. Perhaps you can fetch someone who might be able to help our friend here?

One of the taps bursts, and starts spraying water all over the place.

Oz I'll leave this with you.

Oz hands Jo the knife and leaves.

Jo I really don't feel very well. I really think I need some help, you know? I really think I need some help. Please. I really think what I need is someone to help me? Someone please help me? Please I don't feel myself. I don't feel like myself. I don't know who I am. WHAT THE FUCK IS GOING ON. I said WHAT THE FUCK IS GOING ON. I need someone to help me now please get me out of this . . . Who am I WHO THE FUCK EVEN AM I please

could somebody just help me I just need a . . . hospital?
I think maybe I need to go to a hospital or I

Is there anyone . . . .

The Four Horsemen of the what?

The Four Horsemen of the . . . ?

Help.

What's

Help.

*Jamal enters. He has cleaning equipment and starts to
clean the room, not seeming to notice that anyone else is
in there.*

Jo Who are you?

Jamal Cleaner.

Jo I don't need a cleaner, I need a . . .

*Jo starts having a seizure. It is brutal and shocking.
    As he falls to the floor, Hunter, Frank and
Ola transform into Paramedics before our eyes. They
crouch down and tend to Jo expertly. The music is
peaking.
    The Paramedics carry Jo out the room.
    As the door swings shut behind them, we hear the
sound of a crowd cheering. The music fades away.
A stillness comes over the space.
    Jamal is stood there, mop in hand.
    He looks at the mess around him: smashed cubicles,
broken taps, graffiti. He carries on with his tasks.
Scrubbing and fixing.
    Eventually, Fin, also with cleaning equipment, walks
in . . .*

Movement Three

Fin Sorry. Bus.
  God. Animals.

We watch as they go about their work.
  The floor is cleaned.
  Toilet rolls replaced.
  The graffiti scrubbed.
  It's beautiful in its own way, and takes some time. The two men work in a kind of harmony.
  Were they in a different context, we might mistake them for dancers.

Did you see it?
  Guess you were working weren't you yeah.
  God. He was magic sort of picked it up on the edge of his own box and took it round five people you couldn't believe he was actually doing it the way he was moving it was like he was made of silk but also of steel.
  You were working though yeah I suppose.

They have finished their job by now. The damage is still visible, but the room is in better shape than it was. The scars are there, but the wound has healed a little.
  Jamal leaves.
  Fin looks around. Proud. He leaves.

,

,

,

Then, from off, we hear two voices. They are muffled at first, but get louder as they approach the door:

77

Stepson (*from off*) You sure you've got everything you need?

Stepfather (*from off*) Your mother packed the bag

Stepson (*from off*) And you know how to do it all?

Stepfather (*from off*) Just about.

Stepson (*from off*) Right. Wow. Okay. Where even is it?

Stepfather (*from off*) I think that's the ladies'

Stepson (*from off*) So maybe it's . . .

Stepfather (*from off*) That's the disabled

Stepson (*from off*) Maybe you can go in there?

Stepfather (*from off*) No you need this key and I . . . Let's just . . .

> *The door swings open and the Stepson comes in first.*
> *He looks around the room.*

Stepson It's empty.

Stepfather (*from off*) Good.

Stepson Do you need a . . .

Stepfather (*from off*) Yes, thanks.

> *Stepson leaves and re-enters. This time he is helping the Stepfather, who struggles to move without help.*
> *The Stepfather is half-dressed in a Father Christmas costume. He is sick, and easily loses his breath.*

Stepson Hold on I'll . . .

> *The Stepson collects a big bucket left behind by the cleaners.*
> *He flips it over and helps the Stepfather to sit down.*

Stepfather Just give me a . . .

Stepson Of course, of course

Stepfather I'm sorry about this

Stepson Don't be silly you don't need / to

Stepfather I know I don't need to, I'd like to. I'm sure this is the last thing you want to be doing on a sunny afternoon.

Stepson We don't need to . . .?

Stepfather Oh, no. If it's leaking it'll . . . Just give me a second.

He catches his breath. The Stepson is not quite sure what to do.

You okay?

Stepson Me? Yeah, yeah course.

Stepfather Lovely day isn't it?

Stepson Mm-hm.

Stepfather This part of the summer always gets to me. It's all there, isn't it?

Stepson Sure.

Stepfather Right. You got the stuff?

Stepson Yeah it's all in . . .

The Stepson takes a bag and unzips it.

Stepfather Pass the wipes.

Stepson Are they . . .?

Stepfather The blue I think. Or the green. She went through it all so quickly I haven't exactly mastered it yet.
Yes those.

The Stepson passes the wipes over.

So hopefully we can just empty the bag as usual and then job's a good'un.

(*Picking up on the Stepson's energy.*) Bag. You don't like me using that word, do you?

Stepson Sorry I . . .

Stepfather You're okay mate.
You remind me of your mother when you look at me like that. That sounds strange I imagine. But it's true.
Let's have a look. Help me off with this will you?

The Stepson helps the Stepfather off with some of his costume. This takes a while. They get in a bit of a tangle. It's tough work for the Stepfather. At some point they probably laugh a little at the absurdity of it all.

Right.

The Stepfather takes a colostomy bag out from his waist band and starts to inspect it.

Shit. I think . . .
Yeah. We're going to have to change it.
Have you got the time?

Stepson Quarter to.

Stepfather Okay. Good, good.
Well. It looks like you're going to learn a thing or two today. How does that sound?

Stepson Fine yeah fine.

Stepfather I'd really like to be there when they arrive. It's very important for me. So we should do it quickly but it can't be rushed, if you understand what I mean.

Stepson Mm-hm.

Stepfather I've always wanted to get to know you better mate. And trust me. This is not how I imagined it happening. But let's go for it, huh?
Best if we go over to the . . .

The Stepson helps him into a cubicle. The seat is lifted and he sits down on the toilet. The Stepson crouches in front of him. Door open so we can see them.

Help me off with these would you.

He helps him take off his Father Christmas trousers.

Hot out there isn't it?

Stepson I suppose if you insist on wearing a Father Christmas costume in July, then yes, it does feel hot.

They laugh.

Stepfather Pass me the little thing that looks like a bin bag.

He does.

Okay. So we wrap it around here, and then we clip off the old one. There might be a smell. Can you deal with that?

Stepson Uh-huh sure I just got to be back / for

Stepfather Good boy.
Sorry.
Don't mean to call you 'good boy'. That probably comes across as quite patronising. It's what I used to say to my kids. Force of habit.

Stepson Uh-huh.

He unclips the colostomy bag and puts it into the disposable bag.

Stepfather If you take this . . .
Great.
And now I just have to pull this bit off . . .

He lets out a sharp sound. Something is hurting him.

Sorry I . . . If you could just . . .

Stepson Yeah should I . . . ?

Stepfather Yeah please just for a . . .

The Stepson quickly moves away from the cubicle and closes the door. He stands outside and waits.
The Stepfather grunts with pain.
The sound of a fist hitting the side of the cubicle.

Stepson Shall I get Mum?

Stepfather What?

Stepson Nothing

Stepfather It's still very sensitive is all. Push the stuff in would you?

Stepson slides the bag of things under the cubicle.

Stepfather What a dying old cunt I am.

,

,

I'm just dealing with the stoma now. Do you know what that is?

Stepson I don't / no

Stepfather During the surgery they basically invert a little piece of your intestine and then it passes out through the abdomen and it hangs out. Sort of like a nipple. Well sort of like a nipple and an arsehole in one. I'm just cleaning that. And then I'll put the new bag on.
Sorry that was –
It's easy to forget that people don't . . .
It's a godsend for me, this thing. It's improved things like you wouldn't believe. So I forget it's not something other people are comfortable talking about. Because for me, it's basically the best thing ever invented. I'll be able to experience the summer.

Stepson Going to be nice to see the others / isn't

Stepfather Ah. Death. The only thing you want to speak about less than my colostomy bag.

Stepson No I didn't mean to . . .

Stepfather That's alright mate.
I'm cleaning it up now. With sterilised wipes. If you're interested.

Stepson Uh-huh

Stepfather You know it's only this last year I think I've actually paid any attention to the fact I've a body. Strange that. It took removing my anus to make me realise I ever had one.

The Stepson laughs at this.

Stepson Sorry. I don't mean to laugh.

Stepfather It was a joke. I'm glad you laughed.

Stepson I've just never heard you use the word anus before.

Stepfather ANUS.

Stepson ANUS.

They chuckle.

Stepfather You've been very good to your mother through all this. She's going to need you very much when it happens.
And I know I'm not your dad. But I do have an order for you.
You still there?

Stepson Mm-hm.

Stepfather Stick close to her, alright?

Stepson Yeah
Course.

Stepfather Good man.
They're beautiful, by the way. Your little ones.

Stepson Thanks.

Stepfather They're lucky to have you for a dad.
(*in pain*) Oh blimey . . .

Stepson You okay?

Stepfather Fine, fine. You know you only really learn how acidic shit is when it's dripping down your stomach.
I'm sorry mate could you

Stepson Yeap

Stepson opens the door.

Stepfather The new bag. It's that beige thing with the clip. Can you . . .

Stepson Sure

He rummages through the bag, collects the new colostomy bag and hands it to him.
The Stepson goes to close the cubicle door.

Stepfather It's alright you can
The graphic bit's over

The Stepson takes his phone out and starts to scroll, distracting himself.

Stepfather What a mess.

Stepson Huh.

Stepfather What a mess.

Stepson Oh. Umm. You're not a mess.

Stepfather What? I didn't say I was a mess I...

Stepson What?

Stepfather I said

Stepson Oh I

Stepfather It's just important to me, you know?

Stepson I know

Stepfather It's something my dad did. And for all of his fuckery it's a nice thing to remember him by. And my own kids . . .
Well.
They've other memories that I think it's too late to try and replace with something like this.

Stepson Mum explained

Stepfather Right. Hopefully me dressed up as Father Christmas on a blazing summer's day won't be too surreal an image for them to hold on to.
This sticking it on bit's a pain in the arse.

Stepson Pain in the stomach.

Stepfather There you go. Getting the hang of it.
Wipes?

Stepson hands him wipes.

'

Stepson Thank you.

Stepfather I'm sorry?

Stepson I've been wanting to say thank you. For a while. It's the happiest she's ever been, this last year.

Stepfather Sorry could you . . .

Stepson Sorry yeah

The Stepson closes the cubicle door and stands outside waiting.

'

,

,

Stepfather It's been my happiest year too. I've felt *in* myself. Inside of my body. You know I'd never really enjoyed sex before.

Stepson Wow

Stepfather It's alright it's alright come on you can deal with it

Stepson It's my mum

Stepfather I know.
   I'd never really got the hype. With sex. You know I did it. Obviously. But I never understood all the palaver. All the art made about it. The songs. All the fuss, you know? That drive that other men seem to have for it. That sort of animal glaze that comes over them when they see a . . . Not me. I'd always assumed it was more . . . something for women? The pleasure of it. That that was a kind of female thing. All the touching and the moaning and the . . . Anyway I assumed that that sort of made sense? In evolutionary terms. I mean I wasn't chaste or anything but it was just not something I worried about. I existed from the neck up. And then every time I did get into it. Fucking, I mean. Well. It always seemed to go wrong it always seemed to spell destruction. Like a shit version of Midas. Anywhere I put my nob turned to ash. I suppose I've always thought of myself as someone capable of very great destruction. Like a bull in a china shop. So on some level, subconsciously, I'd shut that side of me down. As a kind of . . . self-preservation? I don't know. Maybe that was what it was about. Fuck knows. But I thought I best not worry too much about the whole bodily side of things. If you had asked me if I could download myself, you know, or be one of those floating heads in a jar . . . I'd have taken that.
   And then I met your mum.

86

And it

        it

                it all

  just

turned me inside out.

Old bloke making discoveries a sixteen-year-old should be making, how pathetic is that?

But it was like a revolution. Like a revolution in my . . . My soul was . . .

I was rearranged. The world rearranged itself around her. It felt so soft to be with her. And I remembered I had a body. Maybe for the first time since climbing trees with my brother as a kid. As a very young kid. The playfulness of it all. Of being able to throw myself up onto a branch. I wasn't a brain attached to a body back then I was all body, I was all brain, it was all me and I could fling myself up into trees and it was magnificent. And I had forgotten entirely about all that. Until I had sex with your mum and I remembered that I existed as a human animal. From the neck down.

So much secrecy. So much hiding. And then . . .

        She prized me open.

  '

One of the side effects of the surgery was a loss of nerve activity to my penis.

So we haven't . . .

I haven't been able to . . .

The doctor said it normally takes about six months to return. And well I've got . . .

Probably won't happen again, with the time I've got.

Shame to have your awakening just before the end. But I suppose some never get it at all. But God. If I could bottle up those few months we had . . .

The conditions of my teenage years weren't exactly conducive to self-discovery. I do wish I'd met your mother earlier. It's hard not to spend the days I've got left thinking about what might have been.

,

Come on. I'm done in here. Give this weird old stepdad a helping hand would you? And I promise never to talk about shagging your mum ever again.

The Stepson opens the cubicle door. He helps the Stepfather to his feet and takes him over to the sink.
The Stepfather washes his hands. As he washes, he counts under his breath.

Never got out of that habit. Counting as I wash.

Stepson You want a hand with the . . .?

Stepfather nods.
The Stepson gathers the rest of the Father Christmas costume and starts helping the Stepfather get into it.

I thought you were Jewish.

Stepfather He works Christmas Day. I've always thought of Father Christmas as a Jew.

He keeps dressing him. It's full of care.

You must let the world in.

Stepson I'm sorry?

Stepfather Remember to let the world in, whilst it's still there for you.
Hmm?

Stepson Mm-hm.

Stepfather You really must let the world flood in. It's not easy. And when it comes, it's not all good. But you must let it flood in.

You see you must submit to something bigger. It's not a grabbing it's a kind of letting go.

Stepson Yeah we should probably –

Stepfather And you've a body, kid.

Stepson Kid is pushing it a little

Stepfather When you get to my age your definition of kid is somewhat transformed.

By now the Stepfather is fully dressed. It's the full thing: stuffed belly and beard and all.

Look at me.

The Stepson takes his phone out.

Put your phone away.

He does.

You've a body. Don't forget that. You've a body that is strange and strong. That has the potential for great violence. And great tenderness too.

They stand there looking at each other.

,

Stepson They'll be getting here any minute.

Stepfather Right.

Stepson Shall we?

Stepfather You know I might . . .
You go ahead mate. Just give me a minute, would you?

Stepson You sure you can . . .?

Stepfather I'll be fine. Feeling much stronger now.

Stepson Great I'll . . .

Great. Yeah. Well.

Thanks

        Uh-huh

            I just yeah

      Well sorry I

              I'll

                    yeah . . .

Stepfather Yeah.

The Stepson leaves.

The Stepfather grabs his belly and lets out a sigh of pain he's been holding in. He scrambles a little for the upturned bucket and lowers himself down onto it with great difficulty.

He takes some time catching his breath.

Then, from a cubicle, the cubicle the Boy was in in the first scene, we hear the sound of a chain flushing. The Stepfather turns and watches, surprised.

The cubicle door swings open. The Boy walks out. The Boy is played by a new actor who we haven't seen before. This actor should be a child.

He wears a Power Rangers T-shirt and moves with the unconsciousness of a happy kid.

He goes to a sink, gets up on his tiptoes and washes his hands meticulously, counting the seconds as he does.

He finishes. Looks around for something to dry his hands on. Decides instead to use his T-shirt.

He looks at himself in the mirror. He's surprised by his reflection. He turns, looking at the shape of himself.

Stepfather Hello.

The Boy turns. Looks at the Stepfather.

Boy Who are you?

The Stepfather looks at the Boy. He considers answering.

,

,

And,

Blackout.

End.

Acknowledgements

To the very many people who made this play possible.

But in particular, to Jay Stull, Keenan Tyler Oliphant, Lucy Kirkwood, Sophie Grant, Jordan Mitchell, Ashley Martin-Davis, April De Angelis, Gill Greer and David Luff.

To Jessica Stewart.

To Dinah, Lily and Jodi at Faber.

To Maanuv, David, Calvin, Matthew and Tom, for your courage.

To the extraordinary James Macdonald.

And to my teachers David Henry Hwang and Lynn Nottage, who show me the way.

But most of all – to Mum, Dad, Josh, Dan and Laura. Sitting around a dinner table with you was the best education a writer could get.

Boys on the Verge of Tears

By Sam Grabiner

Boys on the Verge of Tears was first performed at Soho Theatre, London, on 11 April 2024

Boys on the Verge of Tears
by Sam Grabiner

Cast

Matthew Beard

David Carlyle

Calvin Demba

Tom Espiner

Maanuv Thiara

The part of 'Boy' was performed by **Edward Butler**, **Callum Knowelden** and **Aiyden Manji**

Creative Team

James Macdonald   Director

Ashley Martin-Davis   Set & Costume Designer

Peter Mumford   Lighting Designer

Ian Dickinson for Autograph   Sound Designer

Zoë Thomas-Webb   Costume Supervisor

Amy Ball   Casting Director

Enric Ortuño   Intimacy and Fight Co-ordinator

Tom Nickson   Production Manager

Claire Gerrens   Lighting Associate

Alex Kampfner   Assistant Director

Clióna Roberts, CRPR   Press & PR

Sally McKenna   Company Stage Manager

Olivia Kerslake   Deputy Stage Manager

Jasmine Dittman   Assistant Stage Manager

Eve Allin   Associate Producer

Cast

Matthew Beard

Matthew received a Tony nomination for his performance in Skylight, directed by Stephen Daldry. He played Edmund in the West End in the Young Vic's critically acclaimed production of Long Day's Journey Into Night opposite Jeremy Irons and Lesley Manville, which was followed by sell-out runs in New York and Los Angeles.

Matthew's performance in And When Did You Last See Your Father? gained him nominations for both a British Independent Film Award and an Evening Standard British Film Award. Matthew's other film credits include The Imitation Game, An Education and The Party's Just Beginning.

Matthew's television credits include Scott Frank's Monsieur Spade (AMC); Funny Woman (Sky); Armando Iannucci's Avenue 5 (HBO); Vienna Blood (BBC); Stephen Moffat's Dracula (BBC/Netflix); and Anthony Horowitz's Magpie Murders (Britbox).

David Carlyle

David Carlyle is an actor and writer, best known for his portrayal of Gregory 'Gloria' Finch in Russell T Davies' multi-award-winning Channel 4/HBO mini-series It's a Sin. He received a Best Supporting BAFTA nomination in 2022 for his work on the series and was also nominated for a BAFTA Scotland Audience Award in 2021.

David will next be seen in Two Brothers Pictures' (Fleabag, Back to Life) comedy Dinosaur, coming in Spring to the BBC and Hulu.

He was also the Proud Scotland Award's Entertainer/Artist of the Year 2021.

Theatre includes: The Tell-Tale Heart (National Theatre); You Stupid Darkness! (Paines Plough/TRPlymouth); The Outsider (L'Etranger) (Print Room at The Coronet); Alice's Adventures in Wonderland (Royal Lyceum Theatre, Edinburgh); The Government Inspector (Birmingham Rep and UK tour); To Kill a Mockingbird (Regents Park Open Air Theatre/Barbican/UK tour); Three Sisters (Southwark Playhouse); Carpe Diem (National Theatre); Victoria (Dundee Rep); Somersaults (Finborough); Yellow Moon, The Monster in the Hall (National Theatre of Scotland & Citizens Theatre, Glasgow); Caledonia (National Theatre of Scotland); Hansel and Gretel (Citizens Theatre, Glasgow); You Once Said Yes (Look Left Look Right, E4 Udderbelly); Dead Heavy Fantastic (Liverpool Everyman).

Television includes: Screw (S2); Buffering (S2); It's a Sin; Bodyguard; Lip Service.

Radio includes: End of Transmission; ANGST! The Teachings of Smart Town; Kitchen Confidential; Behind Her Eyes; The Stroma Sessions; Chernobyl (BBC Radio 3 and 4).

David is passionate about working with charities and is an Ambassador for Tonic Housing – the UK's first LGBTQ+ affirming retirement community.

Calvin Demba

Despite no formal training, Calvin's talent has landed him significant roles on both the stage and the screen. Big screen credits include Idris Elba's Yardie and Annabelle Attanasio's Mickey and the Bear, which made a splash at Cannes in 2019. Other film credits include Kingsman 2: The Golden Circle, Brotherhood directed by Noel Clarke, and Nico 1988, which won the Horizon Award at the Venice Film Festival.

On the small screen Calvin can be seen in Amazon's The Rig. He starred in Mike Bartlett's highly praised BBC One drama Life, and Sky Art's drama Madonna and Basquiat. He was nominated for Young Shooting Star at the Screen Nation Awards, and Best Emerging Talent at the Movie Video & Screen Awards for his role in E4's Youngers. Other credits include Sherlock for BBC One and Babylon for Channel 4. He also appeared on our screens in the hard-hitting, critically acclaimed television film, Killed by My Debt.

Calvin was nominated for the Emerging Talent Award at the London Evening Standard Awards for his leading role in Patrick Marber's play The Red Lion, directed by Ian Rickson at the National Theatre. He has worked with James Macdonald, director of The Wolf From The Door, and Simon Godwin, who directed Routes, which were both shown at the Royal Court Theatre. He has also graced the stage of the Park Theatre in Joe Orton's Loot, directed by Michael Fentiman.

Tom Espiner

Training: Bristol Old Vic Theatre School.

Theatre includes: Witness for the Prosecution (County Hall, London); Life of Pi (Sheffield Crucible/West End – Wyndham's Theatre); Berberian Sound Studio (Donmar Warehouse); Kursk (Young Vic and Sydney Opera House); Macbeth, Twelfth Night and The Winter's Tale (Shakespeare at the Tobacco Factory); Anything Goes and Love's Labour's Lost (National Theatre); The Firework Maker's Daughter (Told By an Idiot/Lyric Hammersmith); Peggy for You (Hampstead/West End – Comedy Theatre); Tombstone Tales (Arcola); The Table and The Puppeteer (Blind Summit); Madam Butterfly (ENO and Blind Summit); The Magic Flute (Complicite and ENO); London 2012 Olympics Opening Ceremony (Danny Boyle and Blind Summit); Caucasian Chalk Circle, Britain's Best Recruiting Sergeant (Unicorn Theatre); Ether Frolics (Sound&Fury with artists from Shunt); Going Dark (London Science Museum, Sound&Fury).

Film includes: Stoned.

Television includes: Chloe; The Crown; Ancient Rome: The Rise and Fall of an Empire; Genii In The House; Perfectly Frank; Anybody's Nightmare; Without Motive; Casualty and The Bill.

Tom is co-founder of Sound&Fury Theatre Company and has co-created and performed in all their productions including War Music, The Watery Part of the World, Ether Frolics, Kursk, Going Dark and Charlie Ward.

Puppetry Direction: Great Apes (Arcola) and Meet Fred (Hijinx Theatre).

Foley Consultant: When Winston Went to War with the Wireless (Donmar Warehouse)

Maanuv Thiara

Maanuv most recently wrapped on Ben Wheatley's Generation Z for Channel 4 and Apple's series Prime Target, directed by Brady Hood. He currently features in the second series of ITV's Trigger Point. Prior to this, he starred in Jed Mercurio's ITV crime drama DI Ray alongside Parminder Nagra. Other recent credits include Will Sharpe's critically acclaimed series Landscapers for Sky and HBO, the second series of Apple's Ted Lasso with Jason Sudeikis and Brett Goldstein, series one of Sky's comedy Brassic, BBC Two's The Boy with the Top Knot, directed by Lyndsey Miller, and series five of Jed Mercurio's Line of Duty.

In theatre, Maanuv most recently starred in Vinay Patel's adaptation of The Cherry Orchard at the Yard, after taking the stage in Indhu Rubasingham's production of The Father and the Assassin at the National Theatre. He featured alongside Andrew Scott in the West End transfer of Hamlet, directed by Robert Icke, and featured in A Passage to India at the Park Theatre, directed by Sebastian Armesto. Other credits include Trojan Horse, which was awarded an Edinburgh Fringe First and the Amnesty Freedom of Expression Award at the Festival in 2018, The Funeral Director at Southwark Playhouse and Approaching Empty at the Kiln Theatre.

Maanuv is a Bristol Old Vic graduate and featured as part of their anniversary performance of King Lear alongside Timothy West.

The part of 'Boy' was performed by **Edward Butler**, **Callum Knowelden** and **Aiyden Manji**.

Creative Team

Sam Grabiner – Writer

Sam Grabiner is a playwright and Boys on the Verge of Tears is his debut production.

James Macdonald – Director

James was an Associate and Deputy Director at the Royal Court for 14 years and was also a NESTA fellow from 2003 to 2006.

For the Royal Court: Glass.Kill.Imp.Bluebeard, One For Sorrow, The Children (& MTC/Broadway); Escaped Alone (& BAM, NYC); The Wolf From The Door, Circle Mirror Transformation, Love & Information (& NYTW); Cock (& Duke, NYC); Drunk Enough To Say I Love You (& Public, NYC); Dying City (& Lincoln Center, NYC); Fewer Emergencies, Lucky Dog, Blood, Blasted, 4.48 Psychosis (& St Anne's Warehouse, NYC/US & European tours); Hard Fruit, Real Classy Affair, Cleansed, Bailegangaire, Harry & Me, Simpatico, Peaches, Thyestes, Hammett's Apprentice, The Terrible Voice of Satan, Putting Two & Two Together.

Other theatre includes: Infinite Life (National Theatre); The Cherry Orchard (Yard Theatre); Night of the Iguana, John, Dido Queen of Carthage, The Hour We Knew Nothing of Each Other, Exiles (National); Who's Afraid of Virginia Woolf?, Glengarry Glen Ross, The Changing Room (West End); The Tempest, Roberto Zucco (RSC); Sea Creatures, Wild, And No More Shall We Part, #aiww – The Arrest Of Ai Weiwei (Hampstead); The Father (Theatre Royal, Bath/Tricycle/West End); Bakkhai, A Delicate Balance, Judgment Day, The Triumph of Love (Almeida); A Doll's House Part 2, The Way of the World, Roots (Donmar); The Chinese Room (Williamstown Festival); Cloud Nine (Atlantic, NYC); A Number (NYTW); King Lear, The Book of Grace (Public, NYC); Top Girls (MTC/Broadway); John Gabriel Borkman (Abbey, Dublin/BAM, NYC); Troilus Und Cressida, Die Kopien (Schaubuehne, Berlin); 4.48 Psychose (Burgtheater, Vienna); Love's Labour's Lost, Richard II (Royal Exchange, Manchester); The Rivals (Nottingham Playhouse); The Crackwalker (Gate); The Seagull (Crucible, Sheffield); Miss Julie (Oldham Coliseum); Juno & The Paycock, Ice Cream/Hot Fudge, Romeo & Juliet, Fool For Love, Savage/Love, Master Harold & The Boys (Contact, Manchester); Prem (BAC/Soho Poly).

Opera includes: A Ring A Lamp A Thing (Linbury); Eugene Onegin, Rigoletto (Welsh National Opera); Die Zauberflöte (Garsington); Wolf Club Village, Night Banquet (Almeida Opera); Oedipus Rex, Survivor from Warsaw (Royal Exchange, Manchester/Hallé); Lives of the Great Poisoners (Second Stride).

Film includes: A Number (HBO/BBC).

Ashley Martin-Davis – Set & Costume Designer

Ashley studied at the Central School of Art and Design and at the Riverside Theatre Design Course.

Theatre includes: Mary, Jude, Filthy Business, Rabbit Hole, Hapgood, Wonderland, #aiww: The Arrest of Ai Weiwei and 55 Days (Hampstead Theatre); Leonora Christina

(Odense Teater); A Midsummer Night's Dream (Liverpool Everyman); The Last Days of Troy (Royal Exchange Theatre Manchester); The Umbrellas of Cherbourg (Betty Nansen Theatre, Copenhagen, Denmark).

Opera includes: Tosca (Santa Fe Opera); Vanessa (Glyndebourne Festival Opera); The Elixir of Love (Seattle Opera); Giulio Cesare and Egmont (Theater an der Wien); Albert Herring and Owen Wingrave (Theater Lübeck); Macbeth (Opera de Dijon); Francesca da Rimini (Opera du Rhin); Tri Sestri and Peter Grimes (Oper Frankfurt); Gounod's Romeo et Juliette (Santa Fe Opera/Liceu Barcelona); Une Nuit À Venise (Opéra de Lyon/Oper Graz/ROH Muscat); I Capuleti e I Montecchi (Bergen National Opera); Pelleas och Melisande (Royal Swedish Opera); The Merchant of Venice (Bregenz Festspiele Austria/Polish National Opera/Welsh National Opera/Royal Opera House, Covent Garden); Otello, Macbeth (also Palau de les Arts Valencia); and Falstaff (Royal Danish Opera).

Peter Mumford – Lighting Designer

Recent theatre designs: Rock 'n' Roll (Hampstead Theatre); 4000 Miles (Chichester Festival Theatre); Three Sisters (National Theatre); A Number (Bridge Theatre); Far Away (Donmar); The Ferryman (Royal Court, West End, Broadway); 42nd Street (West End); King Kong (Global Creatures/Australia, Broadway); My Name is Lucy Barton (Bridge Theatre & Samuel J Friedman Theatre, New York); Ghosts (Almeida, West End, BAM); Long Day's Journey Into Night (West End, BAM).

Recent ballet designs: Don Quixote (Birmingham Royal Ballet); Within the Golden Hour, Corybantic Games (Royal Ballet).

Recent opera designs: Orfeo Ed Euridice (Hannover Staatsoper); The Pearl Fishers, Requiem (Opera North); Die tote Stadt (Opernhaus Düsseldorf); Falstaff (Greek National Opera); Romeo et Juliette (Teatro del Maggio Musicale Fiorentino); Peter Grimes (Paris, ROH, Madrid); Madama Butterfly (Vienna); Beauty and Sadness (Hong Kong); The Mask of Orpheus (ENO).

He received an Olivier Award for Outstanding Achievement in Dance; an Olivier Lighting Award for The Bacchai (NT); the Knight of Illumination Award 2010 for Sucker Punch at the Royal Court; and the Helpmann and Green Room Awards for Best Lighting Design for King Kong. Peter directed the concert staging and designed the lighting and projection for Der Ring des Nibelungen (which won the South Bank Sky Arts Opera Award) and Der fliegende Holländer for ON; Otello for Bergen National Opera; and Fidelio for Orchestre de chambre de Paris. He was a double 2019 Tony nominee for Best Lighting Design for The Ferryman and King Kong in New York.

www.petermumford.info

Ian Dickinson for Autograph – Sound Designer

Ian is an award-winning sound designer with extensive credits in the UK and internationally.

Theatre includes: The Witches (National Theatre); 42nd Street (Leicester and UK tour); 2:22 A Ghost Story (West End, Los Angeles & UK tour); The Ocean at the End of the Lane (UK tour & Duke of York's); A Midsummer Night's Dream (Shakespeare North

Playhouse & Northern Stage); Cock (Ambassador's); Jerusalem (Apollo, London); Company (Broadway and West End); Hangmen (Broadway and West End); Uncle Vanya (Pinter Theatre, London); The Lion The Witch & The Wardrobe (Bridge Theatre, Leeds Playhouse, West End & UK tour); Translations, Small Island, Angels in America (also Broadway); Husbands and Sons (National Theatre, London); Camp Siegfried (Old Vic); Europe, Elegy, Roots, The Weir (Donmar Warehouse); True West (Vaudeville, London); Heisenberg (Wyndham's); Fatherland (Lyric Hammersmith, London and the Royal Exchange, Manchester); Junkyard (Bristol Old Vic and tour); Before the Party, Uncle Vanya, Children's Children and Mrs Klein (Almeida, London); This House (Garrick, London and UK tour); Absent Friends (Pinter Theatre, London); Love's Sacrifice (RSC); The Nether (Duke of York's, London); The River (Broadway); A Midsummer Night's Dream, All My Sons, To Kill a Mockingbird (Regent's Park Open Air Theatre); The Machine (Manchester International Festival and New York).

Ian was the recipient of both an Olivier and Drama Desk Award for The Curious Incident of the Dog in the Night-Time, which played at the National Theatre and toured venues worldwide. He has also received Olivier and Tony nominations for his work in London and on Broadway, most notably for Company, Angels in America, Rock 'n' Roll, Jerusalem and 2:22. Ian has been a member of the Autograph team since 2009. www.autograph.co.uk

Zoë Thomas-Webb – Costume Supervisor

Previous credits as Associate Costume Designer include: Nye (National Theatre); Groundhog Day (Old Vic); Black Superhero (Royal Court); and Lessons in Love and Violence (Gran Teatre de Liceu).

Previous credits as Costume Supervisor include: Long Day's Journey Into Night (Wyndham's); Hamilton (UK tour); Rock Follies (Chichester Festival Theatre); New Adventure's Sleeping Beauty (UK tour); Oklahoma (Young Vic); The 47th (Old Vic); and Mayerling (Royal Opera House).

Amy Ball – Casting Director

Theatre includes: Hills of California, Lyonesse, Good, Uncle Vanya, The Birthday Party, Who's Afraid of Virginia Woolf? (Harold Pinter Theatre); Nachtland (Young Vic); Hamnet (RSC); Jerusalem (Apollo); Leopoldstadt (Wyndham's); La Cage aux Folles (Regent's Park); The Pillowman (Duke of York's); Medea (sohoplace); Drive Your Plow Over The Bones of The Dead (Complicite); The Son (Duke of York's/ Kiln); The Night of the Iguana (Noël Coward); Sweat (Gielgud/Donmar); True West (Vaudeville); The Ferryman (Royal Court/ Gielgud); The Goat, or Who is Sylvia? (Theatre Royal Haymarket); Hangmen (Royal Court/Wyndham's); Berberian Sound Studio (Donmar); Cold War, Portia Coughlan, Women Beware the Devil, Daddy, The Hunt, Shipwreck, Dance Nation, Albion (Almeida); Consent, Paradise, Stories, Exit the King (National Theatre); White Noise, A Very Very Very Dark Matter (Bridge Theatre); Maryland, ear for eye, Girls & Boys, Cyprus Avenue (Royal Court).

Film includes: Ballywalter, The Unlikely Pilgrimage of Harold Fry.

Claire Gerrens – Lighting Associate

Claire is a lighting programmer and relighter who specialises in programming and transferring/touring productions around the UK and internationally.

Theatre includes: Drop The Dead Donkey (UK tour); Peter Pan (Crossroads Pantomimes, London Palladium); Branwen:Dadeni (Welsh Millennium Centre); Sinatra The Musical (Birmingham Rep); L'Orfeo and The Fairy Queen (Longborough Opera Festival); Margrethe, She Loves You, Atlantis (Musicals.dk Denmark); Spitting Image (Birmingham Rep); The Wizard of Oz, Billy Elliot (Curve Theatre); Cinderella (Crossroads Pantomimes Belfast Grand Opera House); The Best Exotic Marigold Hotel (UK tour); The Upstart Crowe (Apollo Theatre London); The Magicians Elephant, Wendy & Peter Pan, A Christmas Carol, A Midsummer Night's Dream, Romeo & Juliet, Death Of A Salesman, Othello, Hecuba, Titus Andronicus, The Taming of the Shrew, Measure for Measure, As You Like It (Royal Shakespeare Company, Stratford-upon-Avon, London, UK tour and International).

Tom Nickson – Production Manager

Theatre includes: Mind Mangler (UK tour, Apollo, Off Broadway, Virgin Voyages); Groan Ups, Magic Goes Wrong (Vaudeville, Apollo, UK tour); Coriolanus, Standing at the Sky's Edge, Everybody's Talking About Jamie (Crucible); Operation Mincemeat, Ava (Riverside Studios); Dan Howell Doomed (international tour); The Shark is Broken (Ambassadors, Toronto); Persuasion, Private Peaceful (UK tour); Mischief Movie Night (Vaudeville, Immersive, Riverside); Patriots, Inheritance, Impossible (Noël Coward); The Birthday Party, Who's Afraid of Virginia Woolf?, Nice Fish (Harold Pinter); Sunny Afternoon (Harold Pinter and UK tour); Dan and Phil Interactive Introverts, TATINOF (international tour); The Lovely Bones (UK tour); Pressure (Ambassadors); Chariots of Fire, Ravens, Dry Powder, The Slaves of Solitude, Occupational Hazards, Filthy Business, Wild Honey, IHO, Ken, Reasons to be Happy, Rabbit Hole, Matchbox Theatre, Stevie, Hysteria, Hello Goodbye, Race, Death of a Black Man, Fever Syndrome (Hampstead); The Secret Garden (Keswick and York); Much Ado about Nothing (Rose Theatre).

Opera includes: It's a Wonderful Life (English National Opera); Turn of the Screw (Wiltons Music Hall); Midsummer Night Dream, Cenerentola, Manon Lescaut, Belshazzar, Falstaff, Le Nozze di Figaro, Agrippina, The Barber of Saville, The Abduction of Seraglio, Il ritorno d'Ulisse in patria, Carmen, Albert Herring (Grange Festival); Idomeneo, L'Italiana in Algeri (Garsington).

Enric Ortuño – Intimacy and Fight Co-ordinator

Enric Ortuño is a Spanish Fight and Intimacy Director based on the UK. He is a Certified Stage Combat Teacher by the 'British Academy of Stage and Screen Combat', a certified Intimacy Director and Coordinator by 'Intimacy Directors and Coordinators USA' and holds an MA in Movement Studies from the Royal Central School of Speech and Drama.

Theatre includes: Theatre Royal Bath, Bush Theatre, Soho Theatre, National Youth Theatre, National Theatre Connections, Northern Stage, Nottingham Playhouse, Oldham

Coliseum, Iford Arts, Orange Tree Theatre, King's Head Theatre, Jermyn Street, The Yard Theatre, Arcola Theatre, Ovalhouse, Trafalgar Studios, and Theatre503 amongst others.

Intimacy Coordination for: Warner Bros, AppleTV, BBC, Netflix, Channel 4, Amazon Studios, and Sky TV amongst others.

He regularly teaches at RADA, Central School of Speech and Drama, Drama Studio London and Italia Conti, and has taught workshops in Spain, USA, Canada and Germany.

Eve Allin – Associate Producer

Eve is a producer for theatre. She is Executive Producer at Broccoli Arts, a production company making work for/by/about lesbian, bisexual and queer people who experience misogyny. Broccoli productions include This Might Not Be It by Sophia Chetin-Leuner (Bush Theatre, 2024); Salty Irina by Eve Leigh (Summerhall, 2023); Before I Was a Bear by Eleanor Tindall (Soho Theatre, 2022). In 2022, Eve was Associate Producer at Soho Theatre for Super High Resolution by Nathan Ellis. Independently, she is the producer for internationally award-winning artists Jaz Woodcock-Stewart (Civilisation, 2019–2022); Nathan Ellis (work.txt for SUBJECT OBJECT Ltd, 2022–2024); and Jennifer Jackson. Eve is supported by Stage One.

Alex Kampfner – Assistant Director

Alex Kampfner is a multilingual theatre director based in London. She trained at the Royal Conservatoire of Scotland. Her directing credits include About Money at Summerhall; Women with Wide Eyes at Theatre Deli Sheffield/Migration Matters Festival; Celine at the Voila Europe Festival Festival. As Assistant Director: Disruption for the Park Theatre. She has worked internationally, directing in Colombia, Chile, France as well as throughout the UK. A facilitator, she has led workshops in prisons, women's refuges and with young people.

Alex was shortlisted for the Genesis Future Directors Award and longlisted for the JMK Award in 2023. She is a script reader for the Finborough Theatre and the Painkiller Prize.

About the Soho Theatre

Soho Theatre is London's most vibrant producer for new theatre, comedy and cabaret. A charity and social enterprise, we are driven by a passion for the work we produce, the artists we work with and the audiences we attract.

Our roots date back to the early 1970s at the Soho Poly Theatre. A small but influential venue, Soho Poly was radical and relevant, capturing the excitement and innovation of its time. Today Soho Theatre's work is wide-ranging, drawing from this fringe heritage, and adding a queer, punk, counter-culture flavour. We champion voices that challenge from outside the mainstream, and sometimes from within it too. We value entertainment and a great night out.

We produce and co-produce new plays, work with associate artists and present the best new emerging theatre companies and comedians. We have a thriving variety of artist and talent development programmes, artists under commission and in development, and two new writing awards including the Verity Bargate Award for new playwrights.

We work beyond Soho with a UK and international touring programme, and we film shows and create our own digital work that can be seen on our player, on tv and viewed on international airlines. And we are working towards opening our second London venue, Soho Theatre Walthamstow.

sohotheatre.com I sohotheatre.com/player I @sohotheatre

About the Verity Bargate Award

For over 50 years Soho Theatre has championed new writing, from lunchtime plays in the 70s to today's commissions, attachments, writers' labs and awards. Honouring the organisation's co-founder who passionately championed new writing, the Verity Bargate Award is Soho Theatre's biennial playwriting competition. It is one of the longest established playwrighting awards in the UK and the only award to guarantee the winning play a fully staged production.

Sponsored by Character 7 and open to new and emerging writers in UK and Ireland, the award uncovers the best new plays and has helped launch the careers of some of Britain's most established playwrights and screenwriters. From almost 1500 entries, Sam Grabiner's *Boys on the Verge of Tears* is the most recent Verity Bargate Award winner; the judging panel included industry experts James Graham, April de Angelis, Theresa Ikoko and Stephen Garrett.

The 2024 award winner will receive a full London run of the play staged at Soho Theatre, workshops and rehearsed readings of the play in India and USA, and a cash prize. Chaired by Stephen Garrett (Character 7); judges include Anupama Chandrasekhar, Alan Cumming, Moira Buffini and Ryan Calais Cameron.

For more information on the Verity Bargate Award 2024 and other ways writers can connect with Soho Theatre – including workshops, lab programmes, readings, notes sessions, and script submissions – please visit https://sohotheatre.com/artists-and-take-part/

The Verity Bargate Award is sponsored by:

Soho Theatre Staff

Deputy Audience Manager
Sophy Plumb

Assistant Audience Manager
Coco Jackson

FOH Team Members
Mischa Alexander
Ali Erol Arguden
Brenton Arrendell
Auriella Campolina
Em Carr
Geraldine Carr
Holly Cuffley
Jade Dayna Warner-Clayton
Oscar Holloway
Hana Jennings
Omolabake Jolaoso
Takiyah Kamaria
Lee King-Brown
Theo Knight
Tilly Marples
Kit Miles
Paul Murphy
Fiona Oakley
Janisha Perera
Jessica Phillippi
Theo Ray
Rosie Revan
Farshid Rokey
Alexis Sakellaris
Xavier Singer-Kingsmith
Genevieve Sinha
Johnie Spillane
Sami Sumaria
Abigail Timms
Lauren Tranter
Joanne Williams
Ellis Woods

FINANCE, ADMIN & OPERATIONS

Operations Director
Julie Beechey

Head of Finance
Gemma Beagley

Finance Officer
Paige Miller

Building & Office Manager
Stephen Saleh

Building and Hires Coordinator
Rebecca Dike

TECHNICAL

Technical and Production Manager
Stefan Andrews

Senior Technician
Scott Bradley

Senior Technician
Amy Whitby-Baker

Technician
James Furre

Technician
Matt Iles

Technician
Tom Younger

Casual Technicians
Sophie Botta
Anna Brooks-Beckman
Hannah Fullelove
Richard Gunston
Ruth Harvey
Alexander Hawkins
Samuel Hoppen
Euan Jackson
Edward King
Jodi Rabinowitz
Jake Rich
Jemima Rohde
Abigail Sage
Angelo Sagnelli
Hannah Sayles
Jack Scanlon
Natalya Scase
Georgina Trott

SOHO THEATRE BAR

Head of Food and Beverage
Kim Beeching

Bar Manager
Sachi Naidoo

Deputy Bar Manager
Damian Regan

Bar Supervisor
Jack Parry

Bar Supervisor
Cazz Regan

Bar Assistants
Emma Brunet-Campain
Sofia Dixon
Bibin Gopi
Brooke Hall
Benjamin Jones
Marcel Kalisz
Ridoy Khan
Abin Marson
Zara Mehrban
Max Mitchell
Imani Pugh
Purnima Rai
Vanessa Restivo
April Spiers
Maria Ziolkowska

Soho Theatre Supporters

Principal Supporters

Nicholas Allott OBE
Hani Farsi
Denzil Fernandez
Hedley and Fiona Goldberg
Michael and Isobel Holland
Linda Keenan
Amelia and Neil Mendoza

Supporting Partners

Matthew Bunting
Stephen Garrett
Angela Hyde-Courtney
Phil & Jane Radcliff
Jonathan Rees
Dom & Ali Wallis

Corporate Sponsors

Adnams Southwold
Bargate Murray
Cameron Mackintosh
Character Seven
Financial Express
The Groucho Club
Lionsgate UK
NBC Universal International Studios
NJA Limited
Oberon Books Ltd
Soho Estates

Trusts & Foundations

The 29th May 1961 Charitable Trust
The Andor Charitable Trust
Bruce Wake Charitable Trust
The Boris Karloff Charitable Foundation
The Boshier-Hinton Foundation
The Buzzacott Stuart Defries Memorial Fund
Chapman Charitable Trust
The Charles Rifkind and Jonathan Levy Charitable
Settlement
The Charlotte Bonham-Carter Charitable Trust
John S Cohen Foundation
The D'Oyly Carte Charitable Trust
The Eranda Rothschild Foundation
The Ernest Cook Trust
Esmée Fairbairn Foundation
The Fenton Arts Trust
Fidelio Charitable Trust
Foyle Foundation

Garrick Charitable Trust
The Goldsmiths' Company
Harold Hyam Wingate Foundation
Hyde Park Place Estate Charity
The Ian Mactaggart Trust
The Idlewild Trust
The John Thaw Foundation
John Ellerman Foundation
Matters Scheme
John Lyon's Charity
JP Getty Jnr Charitable Trust
The Kobler Trust
Lara Atkin Charitable Foundation
The Leche Trust
The Mackintosh Foundation
Mohamed S. Farsi Foundation
#My Westminster Fund
Noel Coward Foundation
The Peggy Ramsay Foundation
The Prudence Trust
The Rose Foundation
The Royal Victoria Hall Foundation
Santander Foundation
Schroder Charity Trust
The St James's Piccadilly Charity
Tallow Chandlers Benevolent Fund
The Teale Charitable Trust
The Theatres Trust
The Thistle Trust
Unity Theatre Charitable Trust

Soho Theatre Performance Friends

Anna Bordon
Helen Evans
Andrew Lucas
Bhags Sharma
Gary Wilder

Soho Theatre Playwright Friends

Maital Dar
Mrs Emily Fletcher
Liam Goddard
Emma Whitting

Supported using public funding by

**ARTS COUNCIL
ENGLAND**